ADDICTIVENESS: THE PUSHER

ADDICTIVENESS: THE PUSHER

Acknowledgements
To all my friends, my dearest daughter, brother, my son, his wife & daughter.
May god bless them all.

ADDICTIVENESS: THE PUSHER

By: Ce. Dey

Joan Douglas
40 Arcade Road #R
Hackensack, NJ 07601
(201)441-9107

ISBN: 978-1-4269-6870-9 (sc)
ISBN: 978-1-4269-6869-3 (hc)
ISBN: 978-1-4269-6871-6 (e)

Library of Congress Control Number: 2011907150

Trafford rev. 10/24/2011

 www.trafford.com

North America & international
toll-free: 1 888 232 4444 (USA & Canada)
phone: 250 383 6864 ♦ fax: 812 355 4082

INTRODUCTION

As a registered nurse, Ce. Dey is good at what she does.

She has found that not much is mentioned about the seller/pusher of substances. There are the ones who gain notoriety selling. To her, they are the worse for addictiveness. That is the high classes of selling.

Ce. Dey hopes that beside long years of incarceration, these people will receive the help where needed. That is, the mental institutions instead of the prisons.

It is hard to stay away from the criminally expensive way of living. This is another kind of slavery that one is not trained for.

CHAPTER 1

"Oh! Who is it that did this deed?" This is what this mother kept asking herself as she bowed her head in grief. Her son, her only son, was on his way to big disaster, another very big one. There was nothing she could do to stop the trail of drugs.

This viper starts its way outside on the streets, then bore its way on her doorsteps. The chance was quick, with surprise and trickery, then this disgusting viper makes a big leap into her house.

This leech called drugs then storms its way into comfortable surroundings as if they did belong.

With breathlessness and exhaustion, she, the Queen of the house, does the weekly searches, just in case this stranger visits. What did she find in her only son's area? Things that did not belong. With sadness, nervousness, shock and disappointment, she continued her work with tears in her eyes. These tears, they did play with her face, the annoyance of which did irritate her so much further tears did reappear.

A cry of painful hurt, a dejected mother stood by the door of her only son's room. So weak is he, yet he looks so strong. So full of muscles, with a handsome face. What a lovely creature he is, a son who could offer so much, but has so little to give.

Before I continue about Carmen's plight, a poem would be useful to explain her hurt about her terror of drugs.

Drugs Terror

This terror called drugs
Has declared a large war
And we are in firing range.
The destruction that this has caused
Surrounds us for all to see.

The count was high
The devastation great
Lives were taken
How much we could not say.

We all knew this is a dastardly deed.
To take another's life without a word or thought.
A coward it takes to do this evil deed.
To open hell's bowels and spew its contents out.

She asked herself many a time: did she do wrong many years long ago, and work herself to the grind? Did she do wrong by giving him everything and more?

Many a time other mothers told her, but never in her language. How could she understand or pretend to know that which to her was double Dutch?

Ignorance is never an excuse. A mother should be alert. Once she was told her son's name, she should have started looking. Looking for any and everything, and be strong to combat the inevitable.

The anger she felt toward these persons that showed these killers to her son, who in turn became killers to other mother's sons.

Oh! The hurt was quick. The surprise was past. Her son stretched his hand and in a moment jumped among his so-called friends. The jump was quick, and he was caught and made to pay for the crimes he committed. The sentence was long, the payments were huge. It almost broke her back.

He did not hurt. There was no pain. He did not suffer at all. To him it was a holiday to a place like the Caribbean.

There was a send off. The place was packed. The day before the sentencing the music was loud and blaring. There was no sadness or remorse, only a sister, a baby sister's weeping; weeping with sadness at the loss she would feel for months to come. Holding tight to a brother, a brother she looked up to. A brother she loved more than all the world. He was mother, father, and playmate rolled up in one. This sister cried her eyes out, as her brother would be there no more. She held on to him and would not let go until her hands were pried away.

This brother, he cried, and this was the first time his mother had ever seen him cry; real tears of sadness ran down his cheeks. His mother looked for words to say to a son who did the crime, and is now paying for his wrong deeds, with the time.

Carmen then raised her hands to her face, with tears running down at a very fast rate. She said some words of comfort. She said some words for strength.

A Mother's Loss

Who do I turn to
To hold my painful heart?
My baby, the King, with all his strength
Is being taken away in chains.
It feels like death.

This ghastly separation
Leaves a mother hungry
For a glance of a son gone wild.

So cry, my beloved mother.
Let your feelings ease as you cry.
Just show your strength
For your daughter at home
And together you will glow
With a positive force,
Which will pass on to your son,
For a stronger behavior pattern.

CHAPTER 2

The jailer was there, well dressed, with the shackles in his hand, along with the handcuffs all ready to be applied.

This dejected mother moaned within herself as she was the only one there. No family, husband, friend, or foe, only this single mother, all alone, well known to all the courts with her sadness and tears, and the loss of her loving son.

A son who was not hurting enough for the wrongs that he had committed.

Oh, Mother! Please do not cry. You have another child who needs you just as much. She is your baby and a girl, and is hurting just as badly. This sweet little poopsie with fat little cheeks needs a hug and a squeeze from you, Mother dear. So dry your eyes and give me a smile. Be brave and go to your child.

Be strong, dear Mother. Hold on to each other. Share your grief, loneliness, hurt and isolation as you will need that for a while. Then start to pray for a change in him by the time he is ready to start again. Do this with your daughter, chant for yourself and the change your son must make.

You will always remember the clanging of the chains, the rattle of the cuffs, and only a mother alone knows what that does to her, along with the twist it causes in her heart.

This mother says to herself, be strong, Mother dear. Accept your son is weak, for a follower he is, so a society menace he would be.

His ways are still the same. The shame and embarrassment are there as part of his package. You have to be tough to go with this love. You have to be strong to nip this in the bud. Stopping him should be your objective. Trying to change should be your main goal. He must be changed to be accepted into the community, and by everyone.

His mother then noticed that his friends were still around. They had disappeared when he was incarcerated. They returned in full force as soon as he arrived back home.

Their ways had not changed. It became worse. Her daughter knew all the lingo that these young men spoke and translated it to her mother whenever possible.

What can a mother do to protect her children from the evil throngs of drugs? This think is killing the small ones, making slaves of the bigger ones, and causing the older ones to act as fools. A mother knows her sons are safe when they are locked away without the influence of substances.

Everyone thinks using substances is the only kind of addiction.

Selling these is worse. There are sleazes who think they can get away with anything and also hold one over on the police.

These killers are responsible for the deaths of our children, tearing their mothers' hearts as these children are buried. A mother then cries for all the children she has lost, saying to herself while she pleads:

Flee, my beloved babies.
Flee wherever you can.
Hide yourself so you cannot be found.
To become a slave
To that thing that is called Weed.

The names are so numerous
The habits so severe
With destruction in its wake
As you grow along with its use
You know it's painful to give birth
But worse still to stand, and hope
Good men they would or might become.

CHAPTER 3

These sleazes leave our children and babies homeless without anyone to care for them. Thus comes the introduction to the foster homes. Some are good, others are hopeless.

Can't people see that our babies are suffering?

Whichever way you place our children, they are still being killed. This should be placed at the feet of the pushers, sellers, reinforcers, and killer drug lords, who call themselves "brothers" and "dogs" with much love and peace.

She wondered what they were thinking, these people that take away our drug babies and then turn their backs.

It hurts her deeply to think her only son, who had everything, could behave so disgustingly, causing the injury and destruction of our little ones and the community. This habit that he had acquired was a habit with blood on his hands, his head, and his heart. The urge to kill and be rich is what he and his friends decided that was the route to follow.

Is he so weak he needs to follow others? He was taught to be strong and be a man. Instead, he lived on the streets and became a hoodlum, well known to all, a popular street hoodlum.

It's not what you do and who you know that makes you "a man" or "the man." A man has to prove himself in every sense of the word.

Thinking just dressing, being muscular, sleeping with every female that they meet without even protection for themselves and the female of choice at that moment. These men showing their manhood have no control of their body fluids or where it was. "Yak, yak." You disgusting source of male etiquette. You small-minded sellers of substances. Wearing all that gold around your necks, thinking that will make you into gentlemen. Wrong again, dear son and friends.

No matter what you do, you must remember a leopard's spots never change. She then said to her son, "You do not intend to change. You with your street look, your street walk, and glib, fast speaking tongue. Nothing could be achieved."

She bent her head and wept as she had done these past months. Hands in the air, she said:

Oh! My son, please, my son
My first-born into this world
The sweetness that I produced.
Please come back to me.
Come into my arms
So you can be made whole again.

Return to me, oh, my gracious son.
Let me be the one who cleanses you over.
For as any mother who tenders her young,
Always believes the turnout would be fine.
So please, my son, return back to me.

CHAPTER 4

Know that you have given life to a very destructive soul. You have nurtured this disrespectful person into adulthood and watched them as they become monsters who attack those that are weak.

Some also give the very young females to be abused by pushers. How is that for the brotherhood protecting the sisterhood?

Yes, this mother admitted her son is a pusher, and continued. She is hoping for a worse name to call him by. The money, education, and time spent on this child was insurmountable. It is such a shame and disgrace. Everyone in the family and extended family are on the right track in every sense of the word.

She tried to avoid any discussion about him. What could she say about his abilities? He works, has some college credits, does not mean to better himself, and sells his drugs on the streets. He thinks his mother is not aware of this and as his father likes to be left alone, he knows and thinks he can do whatever he pleases.

Mother admits to being angry-spitting angry-that a child of hers is acting very negatively and does not intend to redeem himself.

Whenever she hears the sirens, or a banging on her door, she goes through a terrible panic attack, lasting for over half an hour.

She had also said a strange thought. "At times, I wish he stays incarcerated because I know where he is. He is alive and safe." She is more relaxed and does not have to worry about brawls, the police knocking, banging, or breaking in her door, or any footsteps of people walking.

The father, her husband, does not like to get involved in this kind of trouble. All he thinks about is getting even, or thinking up ways to hurt the family. The mother is only concerned about her son and seeing herself and her son get over his troubles. She is just hostile and upset as her husband did not lift a hand to help their son. He has purposefully left his son outside to burn.

Burning, burning, burning, without even a drop of water to out this everlasting fire. Her husband should be proud, for all that he has prayed for to happen to his wife and son has happened, or should she say, "Come to pass." A son needs a male that he can look up to. Ours never had that.

Fair enough he was put down constantly by his father. She was there and immediately would boost him up, giving him strength and support. Not all men are fathers or father material, just as all females are not mother material. We just have to mix the good and the bad.

She saw to it that her children were well looked after.

Greed is a thing she cannot understand. Her son is this. Just plain greedy. And no one is doing anything to help her. She, a single mother, is crying out in pain, crying out in shame, facing degradation, yet she remains alone.

Where can she go, where can she run?

Can she duck her head in shame or should she cover her head and scram?

These things do not help her, but they do give her release.

Release of all the agony and stress that she has to face each day, and into the lonely nights. The cold, long, wintry nights.

Carmen ponders about her thoughts and wonders about her stressors and loneliness, saying to herself:

Sometimes I cry when I am alone
Sometimes I have to mutter to myself
I also embrace my loneliness
As I try my best to overcome it
But I still have this lonely feeling
That does not seem to go away.
On top of everything
This pit of loneliness
Is trying to get its grip on me
But I will fight it to the end.

CHAPTER 5

What could she do with no strength to fight and no will to do anything? "Should I blame myself for all that has gone wrong," this mother said. She wished she had someplace to lay her head. She continued to say, "Help me, someone, please, please give me a hand."

Her son Zake had strayed very far this time, and there was no one to bring him back. There was no one to stop him in the beginning, much less stop him now. What kind of man turns his back on his son in this time and age? Lift not a finger to help him and stop the crime?

The screaming Carmen felt to let it out would only come out as a shrill or a sniffle with tears. Then the choking starts and she rolled into a bundle of nothingness.

To know that a father would not intercede to protect his son, but boasted at the outcome of what would be. Being happy to see the downfall of someone you once cared for, so that you can float at your poor gain.

Carmen said today she is a broken woman. A woman who is battered, bruised, and downtrodden. A woman who is trying to push her self-esteem again to the heights. A woman who will try to reach her goal one day. A goal that she once had, but is no more.

How can you trust your male partner when they, in turn, make you lose all your newborn treasures, and without a click keep on going?

Carmen then decided to be strong when her son came home. Making the rules stick and never back down. Being strong when it comes to your children. Be firm with your son.

It's with sadness and tears she bowed her head in distress, protesting at the monsters with the name called drugs. These monsters have destroyed the balance and wellbeing of my family as per Carmen.

Today, a mother groans for the spoils she has received from the war on drugs. She continues, "I am sad, sometimes I am depressed at the crumbled mess of ache that befalls me. Yes, there is tough love, but as the court said, at twelve, he, 'my son,' was a child. That was when my son stated to 'push' as it's called on the streets."

At twelve, when Carmen did not know what was going on, she said her son had requested that she not send him to the stores. She never listened. He did say people were coming around him, giving him things. She could not understand what he meant. She listened, but did not hear.

Her husband knew, but choose to do nothing to redirect his child. He only wanted to see how far he could hurt and destroy her. In doing that, he placed a death sentence on their son, their only son.

Zake tries to care, but so much has passed around him. In a sense, he is like Carmen, not close to anyone and would much rather be alone.

He looks so innocent and trusting, but getting to know him is an impossible task. This is something he does not know how to do. He was hurt so many times during most of his young life by his father.

This hurt of her son's
Can squeeze a mother's heart
And wring this mother's blood
To purify her son.
The hurt that he went through
No other one could endure.

Why must our male children suffer, Carmen wondered. The rejection that Zake passed through in his younger life must have twisted into him as if he was a human sacrifice.

CHAPTER 6

Our older men have taken a set on our younger men. They have treated them just as they were treated by their fathers and those before.

How can our young males become men of strength when they are constantly beaten, insulted, made a laughing stock and bear the blunt end of all their father's and forefathers' demoralizing jokes?

Her son had a lot of that from his father as a child. Things build up. Because children do not respond, fathers tend to think things can be said continuously to our sons without responses made by them. Our sons suffer in silence, but then the acting out begins.

"What I did wrong was trying to hold onto my marriage," said Carmen. "Trying to keep a man that did not belong to me, nor wanted to care for my children," she continued. She then said her children, especially her son, has paid dearly for what she had done.

"Now my son has placed his hurt in a destructive stance, and heaven help those that come into his way. Right now he is like the bear with his fangs and big hands flaying. He is geared for destruction, hurt, and combat, very noticeably in his eyes. After being known as a kind, gentle, sweet child, he is now called a monster everyone has to fear.

"One would think my son has a split personality-kind today and blood in his eyes tomorrow."

Carmen admits she loves her son dearly but hates the things he is doing, the hurting of innocent people that have done no wrong and the hurting of herself because of all these hurts.

His father, at this time, is now trying to be friendly and wants to now be called "good father" and "good buddy," implying their son can now trust this man, who had never cared for him before. This man who never supported his son during any of his troubles. Even now he does not even redirect his son. "My son is left loose to do whatever he wants to do," said Carmen. "My grand always said the sins of the father falls on the children. My son is paying for his father and forefather's sins."

Even her mother-in-law, her children's grandmother on their father's side, would reply and say to Carmen:

1. They are your children
2. That is yours (meaning her daughter)
3. I do not have to listen to what you might say
4. She then told Carmen that she only loves "my boy" as she calls Zake.
5. Then to Carmen's daughter: "Even though I do not love your mother, you are my grandchildren. I want to speak to 'my boy.' Go and call him." That was all she said to Carmen's daughter.

What can a mother do whose son is in severe trouble, facing disaster, his manhood to be taken away from him, and his future to that destructive drug called pot, for it is incarceration he will be facing and a long separation he will have.

A broken-down man with no good aim he will become, as he is released from incarceration and probably have crooked footsteps.

The point is, he did not listen, so a child has to pay as everyone did and Carmen continues:

Even the haughty looks
That were observed
Makes one wonder if that look
Was of old time's hurts, or
Unrecognized animosity.
Looking then walking away
With an angry glare
But returned with a stare of perplexity.

She stood and wondered, this is a state of a child going the wrong way, a child who needs quick intervention.

CHAPTER 7

Carmen claimed that she kept her children very close to her so as to avoid heavy drug influences. It was a shock to her when she found out her only son had broken that code and become mixed up in the drug trade.

She claimed her name precedes her in this disaster. She did not know if people were laughing, talking, or sympathizing with her. She knew some were happy about her fall from grace. A very hard fall.

Why would her son not stop this disgusting act? He receives a good salary for a single man. Everything could be done with that. To be greedy and look for a host of other things that encourages further greed should make her son feel ashamed of himself.

"I should now tell him 'fire for shame,' for you have lost your good name. Now you are the cousin of a church mouse as you are now poor because your good name was lost. You were not careful," Carmen said.

Carmen declared she has counted the times she has forgiven. She has counted the times she has screamed. She has also counted the times that she has threatened to put him out. He is her son. What can a mother do or say to stop this man before he breaks her further? What wrong had she committed? What wrong did she do to make her hang her head in shame and have all this grief? A shame that her son had caused by being greedy, a son who is selfish, stubborn, and stupid. A son who thinks he can control everyone by his height, muscles, and weight.

Carmen tried to do things to lift her son's spirits. She tried to plan big moves and business so he could take a part in it. She even tried to make him feel a good and strong person, and not so hurt and angry, but these were all in vain. He stretches his neck and veins to show how displeased she makes him feel.

Sometimes she whispers when he is asleep, hoping he can hear her. Again, this was from Grand. "My son, my son, you mean the world to me." "My son, my son, you're all I ever need." She then kisses him on his cheeks. "Zake is still my son, my baby," she said. She then started crying because of the road that he has chosen.

What a choice for a strong black man. What a waste for a man of color with education.

Sometimes they would sit and talk. And of course, Zake looked so sweet, caring, and loving. She knew he had a lot to offer, and claimed he was gifted. Carmen then said she could never turn her back or cease her feelings toward her son. She bore him and is positive her tender love would always be there. She would never put him out of the house. Yes, the famous hot meal and a bed warm to the touch. "Only I do not cook," she said with a slight smile, "so it must be TV dinners with everything else."

Carmen then said to herself:

A mother's love do stand the end of time.
A mother's love do give her children
The strength to conquer.

I will always give my children
The support I never had.
My love will always be there.
That is why I, as a mother,
Will be there for them.

Oh! Mother love,
Oh! Mother Nature,
Please show me how to use
My strength and support
In the correct way
To safeguard my erring child
An erring child who is on
A kaleidoscope of destructive behavior.

Carmen then shook her weary head in grief, wondering what sin
was falling on her son's head.

CHAPTER 8

The person that brought this curse into our home and through our door has a price to pay when they have passed on. We do believe in Karma. Here is hoping that these people do not return as animals, for our household is one that pets are happy to stay in.

Carmen tries very hard to keep her anger at bay, to stop the stress that consumes her, as these are all negative and causes the immune system to weaken.

When Carmen sees her son with his innocent-looking face, sun glazed bright eyes and smirking lips, she knows he is trying to win her over. She said that looking at him and with all his gifts, he could have become a leader of tomorrow for our children.

Carmen then pleads to Zake: "Oh! Son of mine, be good for once. Please do not let the policemen keep knocking at our door. Stop the cars from coming to our front door, and please keep your friends from gathering at our door. How long, dear son, should I beg for this to be over? How long should I cry for the things you are doing? You do know wrong from right, and what you are doing is wrong. So, please, son, do the right thing."

With shaking head and wringing hands, Carmen claimed her pleadings go to unresponsive ears. She then complains further: "Oh! Dear son, please listen to me. Do the right thing and turn your back to the world of sin as Lot and his family did in their day. To know what you, my son, are doing on the streets, the thought of that sends me into a tailspin, knowing that they would be placed on the streets to disaster and pain.

"Many more mothers would be crying at the losses they would suffer as their children make drugs their master. Another one hits the dust, as well as his good name, down the road to follow in everyone's footsteps.

"So, please, dear son, be there for your brothers, your dogs, as you also call them. They are younger, with no experience for outside life. You must protect them and not lead them down the road where you have passed through.

"You passed through the roads to hell very quickly, and yet, my dear son, you continue on your destructive journey to create havoc and corruption wherever you may go"

Oh, my dear son,
My aching heart pulls
Its muscles carry a strong grip
At the vessels of my heart.

The pain is severe
While my poor bent body
Cries for release
As the pain goes deeper
Into my soul.

Yes, this is the pain that mothers go through
Because of caring, looking, feeling, and seeing
As our young youths go astray.

I will always be there for you,
My son, as you will always be
A part of me.

Carmen then closed her eyes in hurt and pain for a son who is
in the wrong crowd.

CHAPTER 9

"You have disappeared again. You have jumped, and in a moment leaped into a pair of the justices' hands.

They are the ones who can control you. They are the ones you are listening to. Do you think I, your mother, like the way you are treated?"

Carmen then continues, "Do you think I like to hear the clanking of those doors, the ringing of those chains, which includes the handcuffs and foot chains? A mother should never be allowed to see those things.

"I cried for you, my son. For the things you are going through and also for what you have put me through."

To place me into another shame
Taking me down with you.
My heart hurts and bleeds for
Things I cannot repair.
My eyes hurt with pain so severe
For things I cannot see.

"To paraphrase the district attorney's phrase: 'Till hell freezes over."

Carmen continued. "That's forever to me. And so long without my son. A son that you must remember. I turned my back on while trying to amass a fortune of material things. Things that always could be replaced, things that are worth less than my children's lives."

"What," said Carmen, "is tough love? I really would like to know what the old school has to say about that. Would a mother place her child in that situation? I know for a fact these things do backfire. I also know children do not react to that form of discipline. There is a fifty-fifty chance for its success rate.

"Can children go straight after all these things are finished? Can they forgive us for withholding our very strong love from them? Love is supposed to be given very freely, not to be controlled or manipulated."

Carmen said her love for Zake does not falter nor become unsteady. "I started a shower of tears as I saw them start to remove him from the courtroom. Tears running wildly. I cried and cried again, and when I could not control those tears, I screamed and screamed for my loss.

Put it in good stead, a voice kept saying to Carmen. Put it in good stead.

She cried some more and wondered if that would work. She cried and hoped there would be some good. She started planning for his new change and turn-around when he would be discharged.

Carmen started visiting, but could not take it. The thought of seeing a loved one in that orange suit. They leave a heavy imprint on one's mind, even years could not erase. Also, those filthy thick glass cages and unclean phones. That set-up is terrible.

Zake is paying for his mistakes without a complaint. With him one can never tell what he is thinking. "He has good eye contact whenever I visit and tries to make me good in spirits during my visits," Carmen said. She became very anxious and had to stop.

Carmen's life was in total upheaval. She had no idea what to do. She continued, "My children are mine. I tried to keep them together, but have failed in this aspect. I started to pace and never went to sleep. I could not hear a sound without jumping out of bed. At this time, only my daughter continued to visit. The children are close. Siblings are different, regardless of what they stay together. Mothers are the ones who go through the trials." She continued after a pause. "I could not eat, sleep, nor be merry. All I could think about was the younger lives that he had spoiled. Holding my head, I gave a loud groan, hoping that things would soon be better. I started the days and longer nights marking them off just to do something."

Christmas came. His place was bare. Food was there, but we could not share. This destructive force that this has caused left its mark straight through my stomach.

"I continued to hear the sirens and wondered if my son was faring well," said Carmen. "I wondered what did I do wrong with my son and my love. How can one's love go so astray when loving is so right. There should be no wrong. This is learned behavior and comes straight from the heart and to my head."

Carmen did admit to her longing for Zake, but scared to know what he would be like after his incarceration. She was sure he would be better. The family prayed continuously, reminding her daughter Zola, the praying family stays together. "I had a large support with my sister in Florida, her children, close friends and their children. They all chanted and prayed. I cannot stop thanking them."

Carmen tried being calm and composed, but all the time her stomach was churning and gripping continuously. "My nerves were running at a high level. There was nothing to calm me. You see, time went by so quickly it was time for my son to come home."

Carmen sat on her stoop, lost in her thoughts as usual:

Oh! Please be strong.
Show your peeps what you have gained,
What positive thoughts and lessons
You have earned.
Please, my son, this is a new start,
A good start, if you can use that.

My thoughts are jumping frequently.
They have lost their focus
And are now tangible in nature.

So please, my son, be strong
When you are out.
Give the world a large surprise
That you are a strong big brother of color
Who would not give Mom any more grief
To cause her thoughts to be not focused.

CHAPTER 10

Zake was discharged and went straight home. He hugged, kissed, and of course there were lots of tears. Carmen said she noticed her son appeared apprehensive. A few of his college friends were with Carmen and her daughter to receive him.

His nervous tension started immediately. The trusting factor started, the observations and trials. It was a hot time.

Carmen tried to be there for her son, as always, but Zake appeared, according to Carmen, like the slippery eel he was before. He coiled in secret, continuously, the glibness showed. "To me, he had not changed," said Carmen. "The same friends and crowds started coming, the same signs that he showed previously started again."

All of Carmen's friends spoke to Zake, trying to give him encouragement. She also spoke of love and caring, also tried talking about his father and all that happened in the past. It was a dead end. Zake was determined, hard as nails, angry with an explosive temper that was called black rage. There was a lot of work to be carried out. Oh, this uncontrolled urge to hurt, especially when he was very angry. He went into incarceration quietly. A little rebellious, knowing at times he would challenge authority. That's normal for most males. Now he was out. This unnecessary anger that he had cultivated was very frightening.

"Nothing stops him and I did not back down," said Carmen.

Slowly he started to rebuild, gaining strength, getting more support and holding his jobs. "Zake claimed he never had any urges," said Carmen. She knew he was not an abuser. He did not use. He only pushed, which was just as bad and very heavily addictive. She did not believe anyone thought selling was addictive. "But to me," continued Carmen, and also Zake, "that part is worse." As Zake said, no one has ever asked him about his feelings on that subject, but he is sure his other street brothers would agree with him. The thought of wearing those expensive clothes and everything that goes with it should make pushing a number one priority.

Carmen then added her piece, saying that pushing should be a very great addiction, and that is what her son and his friends craved for.

"Fancy clothing never made a fine person. Somehow that seems to escape my son's mind. On top of that, even thought he was signing in on his sessions, I, as a mother, think some group sessions would work wonders. He needed groups: anger management, narcotics group, trust, anxiety-that everyone should have after exiting from incarceration. That is anxiety."

"His activities started to increase. Up and down, here, there and everywhere. He started to go out every two to three hours. On top of that, our doorbell was busy."

Carmen confronted him head on, even though she was hurting inside. She knew he was selling. She also said if she saw any strange car or people around her house or ringing her doorbell, she would call the police. She knew he had believed her this time. She also reinforced that anyone calling would be informed that he was not living there

Carmen gave a deep sigh and continued. "I have reached the end of my plans, new ideas and everything possible that would make my son a better man." She admits not being a harsh person, common, nor loud, but she has tried all of these things to jolt Zake out of his behavior. Nothing moves that young man. Carmen sat thinking of what else could be done to help Zake.

The church is a good place
Where everyone should go.
It brings back stability,
Strength and love.
I know my son would benefit
From such an environment.

The thought of that was positive. Just thinking caused such excitement in Carmen's thoughts. With tears pouring uncontrollable, she only hoped this would assist with the problem of their strained love.

CHAPTER 11

Carmen says nothing moves her steel-bodied son, and admits he is angry and upset with her because she is not making excuses for him. She continued, "He did go through a lot in his younger life, but how long is he going to keep punishing me for the past? At the ending of his near twenties, he should have made some soul-searching of some sort by now."

Carmen strongly believed that her son could have been saved when his father knew he was selling and would not redirect him. "I know my son would have stopped, as he had looked up to his father, even younger than twelve years old." She described how hurt she was at the way Zake and Zola, his sister, had suffered and the heartache Zaka, her husband, had caused the family.

Zake's troubles began around twelve years old. Had Zaka interceded, things would have had a different outcome. Things do not happen in the order we want them to.

Zaka's willingness to hurt and see repercussions was very strong. He looked on quietly with hatred, smirking with disgust, just to see my downfall, as I fought my son's habit with him and tried to protect Zola," Carmen said. "She is our baby, saddened by a father who drinks and plays with fire, and a brother going away and leaving her unprotected. She was in a state of shock and for once showed rage. Rage to both men who were never there for her."

Carmen's strong believe was that parents should protect their children.

"In our case, this was dysfunctional. I do not think another home had this problem. I thought in third world countries what had happened to us, as no one was bothering with us. All these things reminded me of the British and what took place when Britain was leaving as they were going-leaving us with all the different kinds of hurt, pain and different kinds of abuse. We could hear in the distance Britain's 'Never, never, never, shall be slaves.' They left us to our independence into a worse kind of slavery.

"Zaka could not show love and kindness, hence the love for my children and myself was never there," said Carmen. "He locked his love in fierce shelter and would not give anything to his son, Zake, a son who needed a man to understand and to talk to one-on-one. Share and do things that men and sons do together. My son had never had that, although his father was in the house. Imagine turning your back on your two children, especially your male child? Oh, how the children suffer for the sins of their fathers."

As Carmen continued to explain the changes her children went through, she wondered about these things, speaking to herself. She said:

How long must we suffer?
How long must we stand unprotected?
The females of the families are left very exposed
For danger's eyes to behold.
Why look on us,
You evil creatures of wrongful doings?
You wicked creatures of deadly deeds.
Your aim is to hurt.
So you must be stopped
And become a weaker hindrance.

CHAPTER 12

"Today," said Carmen, "Zake is going out," and her heart shuddered.

Was he going to return? Would she receive a phone call from one of his friends saying that he was killed? Would the police pick him up and take him away? Should she sit up and wait until he returned? Would he come home early this time? "Still, I would not argue. I would sit or lay in bed until he returned home.

"One night," said Carmen, "I wandered from my bed and decided to wait on my steps for my baby boy to come home."

Carmen said she fell asleep on the steps. Zake came in quietly, leapt over her and went straight into his bed. He left her curled up on the stairs sleeping. She awoke at six in the morning, jumped up stiffly, her joints very painful as she was not a young chick any more. She crawled up very slowly into her son's room, intending to rest until he came home. There was Zake, in his bed, fast asleep. That almost stopped her breath.

She woke him and quite calmly said, "What do you think, coming in here, all kinds of late hours?"

He responded quite innocently, "Ma, I came in at twelve o'clock midnight. You were very soundly sleeping. I hopped quietly over you. You looked so comfortable that I hated to disturb you. You only now woke up."

Carmen said she cleared her throat and very quietly turned around to depart toward her room. "I was so ashamed. I was caught sleeping on the job, and the little worm did not even wake me." Certain things like that reminded Carmen what a prankster he really was.

"If only Zake could change his way and be the good person he really could be. I know he cares for children, but can he be trusted with the older ones? He has to prove himself to me two-fold before I can say 'yes' to any questions of that nature. Certain things in life you have to be taught. What my son is doing is learned behavior. That part of his education someone else is responsible for. I wish I knew who that person was. Imagine the large amount of innocents they have spoilt. I am longing to meet and know that person," said Carmen. "I can assure you they will then know what a hurting mother is and what a hurting mother can do. They have left me to hurt and grieve as they continue on their way of destruction, pilferage and hurt of further innocent souls. The saddest part is that these people are never caught by the law. Only the small people, like the pushers or the abusers of substances, who pay for the big people who are protected.

"Why can't the law find these people? Or is it a case of Peter pays for Paul and Paul pays for all? I am not going to give my son a label and let him fry in it. As a mother, I try to protect him and pray forever for a change in his attitude," said this hurting mother.

Carmen then said to herself:

Dear Mother, don't you weep.
Dear Mother, stop the wailing.
We give birth to them,
And nourish them,
But their minds are made up
To do wrong.
So, Mother, stop the wailing.

CHAPTER 13

Carmen said, "A mother cries for a number of reasons, and one most importantly is the tears of sadness. The tears of hurting and hoping by a mother whose heart and head are filled with positive changes. As my grand would usually say, 'Always be charitable, learn to have faith in everyone, loving all males and females regardless of whom or what they appear to be.'"

She then said she had tried all three, but the surprise she does feel very deeply. A mother dies when any of her children faces a disaster. She goes through the pangs of labor every time something negative happens to her children. She continues with her grieving process as she tries to control herself from her shudders and panic attacks.

"I now realize that a parent cannot be blamed when a child goes astray. A child does whatever they want to do, when they are out of your sight, and that's the honest truth. The difference being, we were careful. This generation does not care, has no respect, nothing phases them, even if they are caught."

Carmen continued in the same vein: "When I started with my son and his drug problems, I almost lost my mind. I really thought the police were picking on him. How dare they bully and say these things about my good son. My baby. I could not think for one moment they were right. All my teachings, love, support, and talks we had, especially as he was growing. It appears he did not listen to a word that he had heard or was taught.

"Zake knew the good and bad sides. I never spoke to him about selling, as that was not an option. How stupid was I, not to be aware that selling was also a heavy part of addiction.

After all of these accusations and multiple court cases, plus the expense of a lawyer's fees, Carmen said she decided to send Zake away to a rehab center in upstate New York. It was quite far, and she was sure there could be no contact with his drug people. The day these people came and took Zake away for treatment was a very traumatic time for her. Almost all of her past forgotten, unpleasant memories came back.

"I looked at my son's scared, shocked, and very sad eyes. This was the first time he had ever left my side. With tears flowing everywhere, I could not see where I was going. I felt my heart coming through my mouth. If felt as if it was the end of my life. I never knew I would still be alive. My first born. Zake, Zake, my baby was being taken away from me. I stood and watched them drive my Zake away.

"Only one person was waving at my Zake and that was my grandma. My grandma who had passed on. My Dutch grandma. I knew she was by my side. I felt her presence. I begged softly. I asked her to let my Zake be okay. Please look after him. He looked so scared, with pleading eyes.

"I stood and watched as the car disappeared. I broke down and cried. It seemed forever, as I felt grandma's wind on my face, cooling me off. There were no trees around me. It was soothing to me, calming me down, and slowly I stopped crying. I knew my son would return safely. Grandma's spirit was with me. She was a very strong Dutch lady.

She always said she would look after me, even to the end. That's the truth." Carmen spoke to her grandma quietly:

Oh, Grandma, please shower me
With your cooling wind.
Protect us from above.
I always feel your presence
When things go wrong.
That is your way of saying
I am there for you.

CHAPTER 14

Carmen was saying her children were eight years apart. The stomach gripes, headaches, and sadness was too much. The constant appearances of Grandma in her thoughts was a good thing.

"I remember one of her sayings: 'Rachael crying for her children, and they were no more.'

"I called for my grand, who was no more, then went inside my home and became lost in my thoughts of yesteryear."

Carmen continued in this mode, saying she settled and again calmed herself. "Crying in choked sobs, trying to get everything out, this crying would not stop," she said. She was crying for her son who had lost and messed up his life. Gone were the plans for college and all the positive things he had wanted to achieve.

Zake's life was destroyed all because of his wanting to sell substances.

"I kept remembering all of Grand's sayings: 'The burning deck.' My child was all alone and was standing on the burning deck of drugs. That hurt so much. Also, 'the little lost boy.' Because he was lost, he became lost in a maze of drugs and did not know what to do.

"Oh, the pain, the hurt. My head, my baby, and my tummy. I was calling on everyone and everything to ease the pain that a mother feels. This mother hurts for her child."

Carmen declared she took her son's departure as if he had passed on. She settled and canned her nerves in her son's room. She stayed there for the day, until it was time for her daughter to come home. She did not know that her brother was going away.

Calmly and slowly Carmen hugged her daughter and told her. "Together we hugged, cuddled and cried. We comforted each other. She is a sweet child, that daughter of mine. As young as she is, she has the brains, kindness, and sweetness of an older person."

Carmen then went to clean Zake's room. Under his bed she found all his drug paraphernalia. She flushed everything away, cleaned and sat and wondered.

"Where did I go wrong?" And again, "What did I do that twisted Zake's mind?" Of course, I cried and cried again.

"We were not allowed to visit until about two weeks. We went with apprehension. My daughter, his girlfriend, and I.

"The meeting went well. It was a good day. That was the first time he admitted to having a drug problem of pushing/selling. I did not get the impression he thought, as he was not abusing, that it was smooth sailing. Not so. He abused occasionally and that was enough for me."

Carmen looked at him and wondered how she could get across to him the huge wrong he was doing. She decided to fix it in her mind first:

Oh, son of mine
How can you perform
These dastardly deeds
And expect love and kindness in return?
The wrong that you are doing
Will send many to their graves.

CHAPTER 15

"Having the attitude of the streets, he really could have smooth talked his way inside that institution. When my wayward son found that was not working, he became very disruptive. In the end, he was discharged home during the third week. Naturally, he promised me, his mother, the world, and this very trustful mother believed him. He was a changed person.

"That is the convincing part of that disease. The minute Zake came home he went straight to the streets and his drug friends. The anger, surprise, and shock took me all at once. I really should have listened to his counselor. He wanted him to be transferred to Florida. The point was, I had missed him also that I felt it was too far away."

Carmen then said she sent Zake to a private counselor. "He was as stubborn as a mule. He would not give any information regarding his home situation. It was a tough battle. All I knew was they agreed with the same conclusion. Zake was a very angry young man regarding his past and the home situation. Oh, what a life!"

Carmen became ill. Her pressure went up. Her depression became worse. Again she was alone. "Zaka did not lift a hand to help, council, redirect or give any kind of support. It reminded me of a poem Grand had taught us. My grand was a retired headmistress. This poem was My Land of Counterpane. The line I remembered was "I am a giant, great and tall, that sits upon the window sill." I compared myself with that giant because I was alone. I felt tall, strong and invincible. I had to be. I was a single mother," said Carmen, "fighting for my children-my first-born, to save him from incarceration.

"The bills were so high, I could not turn to anyone. There was no one near. I lost so much. Everything I worked so hard for, and might I remind you, all the lawyer's fees, and bails, also the treatment programs.

"Everything went. Our home. Then came the shame and degradation. Everything, even our family name. We were popular. The whole place knew the family. People came calling, friends visiting. You would think it was a wake. Tears, sniffles, blocked noses, along with my never-ending headache.

"My son has passed on to a new, better generation. Stronger, careful, and continues on a stronger passage. I still worry continuously because you do not know these young people can slip back into that selling trap.

Carmen wondered when things would return to normal, and as usual, said to herself:

Can we ever be normal again?
Should we try to keep our heads very high?
Life goes on. A new start is planned.
And the wondering now continues.

Oh, young brother,
Pull yourself together.
Do the right thing, my man.
Pat yourself on your shoulder
When you call yourself a man.

You have now moved on
And are now a man of strength.

CHAPTER 16

Carmen said she personally thinks these young people should continue with their programs, not because we do not trust them, but to let them remember what would happen if they let go.

"As mothers, we try protecting our children from any negative influences, including their good friends and wayward relatives, especially our male children.

"What happens when they can walk and not crawl? They go right back to what we had tried to protect them from.

"It is so hard to bring up your children in the right way when the friends they pick up are those without values and training. Do not get me wrong. I am not blaming any weaknesses on anyone."

Carmen is saying her son is now trying to be independent, but some of the negative friendships are still around. Maybe in time he would leave well enough alone.

"I have noticed he is traveling a lot to games in different states with his friends. Also, for entertainment with his fiancee. Years earlier, he would have never undertaken that event. I just hope he continues in this way. Zake's impulsiveness is at a minimum. I noticed he is thinking carefully before any decision or even talking things over with his sister. I am looking and watching."

Carmen claimed she knew her son was an adult at this time. "To me," said Carmen, "he is still my baby. I will still continue to fight for him and my daughter as long as I am alive." Carmen said at an early age her children did not own her anything. She owes them. As she said, "I do not expect them to give me anything. All I expect is for them to be there for each other, protecting, caring, and nurturing."

Carmen said she would like, if allowed, that she should pass away before her children, but whatever will be will be, or what is dictated. At this time she is taking one day at a time with her son, allowing him to make his own decisions and plans for the future.

Carmen also learned not to impose her thoughts on Zake or force him into any situation. She also listens and never makes any judgments, trying to be truthful and honest. She did hope taking these lines and routes would encourage him and strengthen his outlook.

Carmen realizes Zake has a very bad weakness and tries her level best to give support. She continues to look at her son and says to herself:

Oh, son of such weaknesses,
Your cultivation has gotten the better of you.
It has caused you to do wrong,
To do harm to your fellow man.
What kind of man can do
Such damage to mankind?

Oh, son of mine, please change your ways.
Be good and kind to whomever you meet.
Remember the little ones look up to you
For guidance, support and good role models.
So, son, do the right thing
Be a man, my son.

CHAPTER 17

At this time of her life, Carmen sits and ponders all these problems in her heart, wondering how she could have missed all the numerous signs that she had seen. For example:

1. The very increased activity

2. The constant knocking at her door

3. The angry barking of the dogs and wondering why they were behaving in that fashion.

4. Loud voices, loud whisperings at intervals on the first floor of her house.

She did inquire of her son what was going on, and realizes now that she only
heard what she was prepared to hear, and the rest she blocked out, some willingly, or possibly unwillingly.

She could not understand why her husband, who was usually like a bear with a sore head, was now smiling, looking so pleased as punch, and even humming tastelessly throughout the house, as he knew what was going on.

Even when she was told by her son's principal that if he did not stop what he was doing he was going to land in big trouble. Carmen had asked the principal to please explain and at that, he kept quiet.

She then said out loud, "Why do people insist in talking in circles, without coming out plainly and tell the truth?" Carmen also said she found it better speaking her mind than beating around the bush.

Continuing, she realized the high activity that her son was exhibiting was a sure sign that he was in distress, but she, as mother, was not looking or thinking along those lines. As she said before she knew he was not stealing, drinking, nor doing drugs, as far as she knew. She could not understand what was happening and asked her husband to investigate.

Even in college, when everything came apart, Carmen was blaming everyone for getting her son into trouble, never realizing he was selling there also, among other places.

She realizes now that all the signs were there, even in her home. She had no insight into the great disaster that was to befall her and thrust itself into her home, along with the share of gross embarrassment, despair, the loss, separation, and fall of her son Zake, her baby. Although he was wrong, she knew when he was younger, if his father, as she had said before, had tried to stop this activity, nothing of this magnitude would have happened.

Besides being oppressed by his father, Zake, the son of slaves as foreparents, fell into something that he could not get himself out of. Just as slavery, years ago, was very hard to be pulled away from, this slavery of ownership of controlled substances is also hard to be pulled away from. It swallows everything it touches, and also paralyzes. He was caught in slavery's grip and this time it is a life sentence.

This reminded Carmen of the hell she had passed through as an unwanted imbecile as she was sometimes called. She realized her son was now caught in hell. She continued to talk to herself, saying:

What you, my son, are running to
Was abolished years ago.
Our older ancestors had lost their rights.
Now you, my son, are giving away yours.
You have a different master.
This one will place you in the gutter.
This destruction of mankind
Is worse than anything in our new world.
To hurt, destroy, mangle and belittle.
This thing you call drugs
Will drag you by the head
Into the pits of hell, into degradation.

CHAPTER 18

Carmen had tried very hard to stop her children from becoming close to any drug environment. In the end, this had failed. Her son went smack into the same scene she had tried so hard to protect him from.

She was so upset, taking a pause, she said, "The young make such rash mistakes that usually destroy their lives and futures."

Carmen knew immediately that would happen to her son. Carmen, a mother, wept for that which would always be hers, her fallen hero whom she has to assist and start replacing his footsteps all over again, like a newborn who needs his mother's help.

This was a very painful time for Carmen. The blame was on her. The guilt was hers. She has now learned to search every day and every week, spending time to search and speak to her children, taking back her house and home from her children.

She now realizes that the principal, although he was very wrong, placing her son into the very dirty dumpster to break him, could have used other corrective measures. He should not have been placed into that dumpster where all the school saw and mocked him, breaking his self-esteem, degrading him and taking his manhood from him. Zake made a change and became very angry, very superficial, and was fighting here, there, and everywhere.

When Carmen found out about the dumpster situation she collapsed. She said she knew there would be a fight on her hands. Thanks to the major organization that assisted

Carmen at this disgraceful time, this maltreatment that Zake received was discontinued immediately. The principal admitted to the organization that he made a very bad mistake. To this day, Carmen has never received an apology, nor has Zake.

The hurtful part is that these people would never have placed their children in a dirty, infected dumpster to clean it out, only other people's children. "They have shamed my son," said Carmen, "and ground his manhood into smithereens."

Anger knew no boundaries as Zake became so angry he started fights and got into bad company. His grades were good, but began dropping after his behavior deteriorated. The aftereffects of the dumpster event on Zake were:

1. Low self-esteem
2. No eye contact
3. He cultivated a laugh the like one has never heard.

"I bedded and pleaded with him to change that laughter," said Carmen, as it was a laugh filled with shame."

This principal was evil and never deserved such a trusting position where children of all races were and attended. Carmen was sure, although she is not laying blame on others, if things had been handled differently, Zake would be the kindest scholar anyone would have the pleasure to meet.

Again, talking within herself, she said:
My son, my son,
The hurt that you went through.
My son, my son,
You were young when it started,
But it followed you in every way.
It is time for the chain to be broken.
These crosses need not travel the world with you.
You are a grown man now, my son,
A man that demands respect,
A man that gives respect.
So please change your ways
And make a commitment to yourself.
Today I will make a fresh start
For I am me, and yes, my name is Zake.

CHAPTER 19

Carmen learned, as a working mother whose husband was never around:

1. Material possessions are not as important as we all think they are.

2. Listen to what people are saying. Listen very carefully. Never get hostile, arrogant, angry, abusive or threatening.

3. Always remember, children come first. Be there for them. Never overlook, underestimate, or treat any complaint as minor.

4. Everything is important. Everyone is important.

5. Happiness, love, kindness, faith, hope and charity. These are the things that our children need in this life and even much more.

6. Never doubt your children when they complain. Hear them, support them, and back them up.

7. Know your children. Know them well.

Carmen became a silent weeper when her son Zake went away to rehabilitation, and also when he was incarcerated. It looked like forever. She was so distraught. Zake had never left her side unless he was in the hospital, and even then she would be there with him or his sister.

She never stopped. It seemed everything upset her. For example, the empty room and the empty space at the table. To her, it felt like the loss of a loved one. It felt like death, the silent grave. It felt as if she had buried her son, her first born baby.

Many a night she could not sleep. Many a night she was talking to herself.

A mother's hurt never stops for her children, neither the grief she feels. The pain, the hurt that never goes away. Her thinking process is messed up by all of this. Then goes the worry of what would become of her Zake when he returned back home. She prayed continuously.

Zake's sister became very sad. The hurt showed in her sweet little face. Her eyes were expressionless. Her grief was so severe.

Carmen, as usual, placed her hands into the air, as she was accustomed, to feel her grandmother. This always helped to ease her hurt. She knew her grand had passed on, but still felt her presence whenever her pain was intense. She would then speak to her grand. "Oh, Grand," she cried, "please hold my heart. Please rub this ache away. Just cuddle me, my dearest Grand, and make me whole again."

After her relief, Carmen decided to take a pause, then continue her famous talking to herself about her children. She said:

A mother's love never ceases.
She has made her creations liken to herself.
And protecting them she must
As they are the gifts that she has received
With promises to Grand
And protect with all her life.

CHAPTER 20

Carmen, as a mother, pondered the severe repercussions of addictiveness in her heart. She then listed them in order as they appeared in her mind:

1. Murder of the seller
2. Complete killing of entire families
3. Kidnapping of one or more family members
4. Very long imprisonments
5. Disruption of family
6. Destruction of family
7. Loss of family members by usage
8. Drive-by killings
9. Killings at drug-busts
10. Killings of innocent people by stray bullets in the home atmosphere
11. Accidental killing of babies.
12. Breaking and entering of the homes of drug elements
13. Over ingestion of the drugs, causing a loss of life and/ or paralysis
14. Addicted behavior

She then wondered what would become of her son. What would become of them? She decided to place bars on her windows and special locks on her doors. Carmen got on her knees and decided to give a prayer for help.

Carmen hopes and prays that no one experiences whet she has gone through. To her, drugs are worse than cancer. So please, mothers, beware. Spend time with your children, get to know them, know their friends, their friends' parents. It does not matter how old they are.

See what they have brought into your home. Remember, that is your home. They are only living or stopping there. If they want to act grown or be grown, then let them go.

Tough love is what it is: tough. Carmen admits the hardest decision for a parent to make is to let their child or children go. Always remember the love of a mother can turn a child into a man or a proper woman.

Carmen remains a troubled woman. She continues to be concerned about her son and other family members. She strongly believes a mother's love can overcome everything.

Carmen is a strong believer of mother's love and support.

Talking to herself, she said:

I made them, also sheltered them.
I know I am prepared to go to the length with them.
Oh, wayward child,
Take my strength to make yourself whole
You were born to lead, so lead.
You were taught
To never turn your back on your enemy.
So face your new problem head on.
This will give you courage
As you will become
A man who was there and came back whole
And is now taking one day at a time.
Never long for expensive things
That your money can not afford.

CHAPTER 21

Carmen ponders these negativities: What would her accusers think? The disruptive, unsettled life that this has caused families is very sad to behold. For example:

1. The breaking of the home, leading to counseling, divorce, all because of this substance called drugs.
2. Assaultive behavior
3. Abusive behavior
4. Threatening

As if this is not enough, this leech, this cancerous-eating, infectious killer tries to take over the entire neighborhood. It then becomes the land of infectious drugs. The entire place becomes vice land, drug land. No one is safe, not even our little loved ones.

The most hurtful part is that the majority of our children who are involved in this rot are from good homes, some with strong upbringing, good grades, with fathers in the homes.

I do not think because fathers are in the homes heavily involved with everything in the house that the child or children would not be involved with substances on the streets or the child or young adult would not become very street wise, whether male or female.

Everyone seems to place blame on the single female parents. What have they done or whom have they hurt to become the punching bags, doormats and condemnation for everyone in sight?

What is the suggestion here? Should being single prevent mothers from becoming good parents? Next, you will be saying, no, they should not become pregnant or should the population be saying take these babies from their mothers. The foster care situations would be very busy placing all those children.

What this comes down to is the plan for making these mothers the cause for populating their country, with not even receiving a measly penny. Of course, the ethnicity would not count, but everyone knows better.

The crime is committed. What is the first thing we hear? This is the way it goes:

1. This comes on the television: He is black. That's understood. If no color was described, that is also understood.
2. Of course, the next thing you hear, and this is the hard one that is used. Even the attorneys lean heavily on this one:
   a. the ghetto area
   b. living fatherless. Single mother on welfare with lots of children.

A couple of things happen here: The education process is discussed everywhere. Even those that are not educated have the gall to cast such aspersions on these dear, kind, loving mothers and their situations.

What no one says is: a) how hard these mothers have to work, and b) no one talks when one drops and never gets up. All we hear is 'so and so's mother has passed.' Why can't it be the fathers dropping from stress.

Carmen then says to herself:

Oh, to take the blame for all
Is a painful hurt most women go through.
Tearing us to bits is something
That the population enjoys doing.
Everyone decides to much off small pieces
And soon there will be no more.

CHAPTER 22

What about the father figures? No accountability at all. No one asks about fathers: what life they led, what they are doing. It is as if these mothers became pregnant by just wishing it.

The only time it appears that fatherhood counts is when something important happens. Yes, our children would claim my mother does everything, knows everything, and is there for them, but that does not mean our sons are fatherless. The fathers are there, use their names, and stop this single parent bashing.

Find these fathers. Everyone can find our children's fathers when child support is to be paid, so find them. Find them when our male children/male young men are in trouble. We, as females, bring them into the world, nurture our boys, would die for them, but now society is using our softness as weakness. We are not strong enough to bring up our male children. As everyone says, it's a man's job. I thought everyone was involved.

Let us count how many famous strong females there are with children.

1. Years and years ago, there was the great Victoria, Queen of England. We now have the present monarchy. Not to forget the person who molded her as a child, her dear mother, whom the world loved. We then have her sister, a single parent, and her daughter, that is, the queen's daughter, a very strong individual.

2. Not to mention the female former Prime Minister of London, whose female strengths brought a lot of support to London, England. She was a very wise ruler/Prime Minister.

3. The very great Madeira Gandhi, a great ruler, who aged with dignity and ruled with an iron fist, like any male in her country who ruled.

4. What about the matriarch of our famous family in the United States? What a very strong lady. She gave birth to all those strong

men, strong rulers, strong followers, then passed away very gracefully. I was always taught that it is a very strong woman who gives birth to male children, some of whom become rulers of countries, heads of state, doctors, nurses, policemen, lawyers, judges, and much, much more. Although we know their husbands plays a part, but history only mentions the menfolk as husbands of so and so.

We females should roar at the injustice that is placed on us as soon as our young, strong male children happen to become involved in the famous system. This system is supposed to help everyone, especially our system.

One tends to hesitate, due to the distaste and shame that others look down on. Others say the judges feel happy if both parents appear in court. I wonder how he feels if only a single parent, a female, goes. Does he blame the mother for her son's downfall? Would he look down on her as she is a lowly female who cannot control herself, her life, plus her children?

Carmen cried and said to herself:

Oh, please do not be harsh
On us single mothers.
Please treat us with respect
As we respect and bow down to you.
We have always held you in great self-esteem.
So please, judge, do not be hard
On us single mothers.
We are not responsible for our future.

We never realized that our mates for life
Could never endure the trials and tribulations
That go with a home, wife, children,
And, if possible, a pet.
So please, dear judge, do not judge
Our sons because of his parents' mistakes.
He is an individual, a very strong son.

CHAPTER 23

I have never heard anyone cast aspirations on their own child-rearing habits, so why cast any on a single mother?

"I wonder who came up with the idea that children must be raised by the male element for them to be strong and free of crime," said Carmen. "I have learned at an early age that it is not the parent figure that counts, it is the person's mind. Some say genetics. I can understand," said Carmen, "the feelings, desolations, sadness, and hurt that others in my position have felt on our partner's lack of interest to our sons. Some husbands do that, and if they are honest with themselves they would admit to same.

"The need to hurt, punish and destroy the female partners is prominent in our male counterparts. The children are destroyed just to get at their mothers. No one thinks of this. My son's background was never taken into consideration. No one asked me anything," said Carmen.

Carmen wondered what she had to do to show her son had not lacked good home training as was portrayed during his trials. He was not a street thug. He was somebody's child. A child growing into an adult, who made a wrong turn.

No one should try to break another person's child because they have the power to be over them. The system takes our children and young adults who err, but have they changed after they have spent such a long time incarcerated?

Carmen cries constantly as she realizes:

1. Who visits her son on visiting day? She does.

2. Who goes to court daily with her son? She does.

Where are these men, these figureheads? What roles are they supposed to play?

The court loves to have both parents, so the courts should insist that both parents should appear together.

It is embarrassing to stand in court alone, knowing full well there is a father figure who decided not to make an appearance, even though he knows a child's life, his child's, is in peril, and the courts want a front of unity showing.

This time, tears were rolling down Carmen's cheeks. She wondered aloud:

Why! Why! Why!
Why do you look down on me?
Is it because I am a lowly female?
Don't you recognize a strong fighter,
A fighter whose strength was
Gained from her ancestors?
A fighter who is a mother,
A mother who fights for her children
Regardless of their ages.

CHAPTER 24

What held Carmen in a grip of continuous pain, hurt and stunned shock was the way her son Zake was treated at one of his arrests. He was surrounded by the police. He had two other friends with him. They were in a park. It was very bright on a summer evening. The police made them:

1. Strip off their trousers
2. Pull their shorts down to their knees
3. Bend over with their buttocks in the air

The police then made rectal searches on the ground in the park in the city. The police felt justified as they were "pushers" and were killing people. To the police, these men were not humans, so they could be treated worse than any stray cur on the street. They do burn curs at the ASPCA if unclaimed.

Carmen maintained they were still human, with mothers, siblings, and many family and extended family members.

The law could redirect in so many different ways, but never with brutality, without dignity, and without bestiality.

Whenever Carmen asked Zake about that particular subject, he would always reply, "I do not want to talk about that." He then would become sad and withdrawn, and kept himself very withdrawn. She now leaves that part of confidential talk alone. It is very painful to this day.

Not one of the police could redirect the other. They all went along with their savage searches on those young men's bodies.

Zake never made a complaint to anyone. He was too embarrassed to have this kind of search be broadcasted. He also did not want anything happening to him suddenly. His friends were also afraid of retaliation from the "man." This was one time the police kept their lips sealed. The famous "Blue wall of silence."

"As a mother, I can still feel the pain of what was carried out on my child and his two friends. So it's quiet I must stay," Carmen said breathlessly. She continued:

Oh, Father, heal our souls.
Touch us to wipe away the pain.
Our tears are continuing to fall like rain.
Please cleanse and keep the souls of all
Clean, fresh and pain free.
Our mothers, they have suffered
And it is telling on their souls.

CHAPTER 25

It came suddenly, without any warning, even though I had lived with this fear all these years. This sister could not accept the court order.

Carmen screamed, screamed, and screamed again. Ah, this pain, this pain reminds me of death. Sudden death. A quick cut, quick separation, and without a thought sadness crept in and into a past mode Carmen's silent thoughts began:

Oh, another milestone, a very big one.
Again I am alone with hurt, anger, and bitterness.
Mother dear is longing for what she could not have.
She is longing for someone she could not keep.

Now crying, using all my tears because of my child.
How can a mother accept the enforced departure of her child-a
son.
You cry a little, think a little, and protest a little.
Then maybe this kind of longing might ease a little.

If I could live my life over, the things that I once did would be set aside to reinforce all positive teachings so as to educate our loving children into the good way. Letting them know that life worth living is life worth having.

The phone rang. It was a quiet morning at ten o'clock on Tuesday, June 7th.

Quote from the caller: "May I speak to Zake, please."

My son came, then returned to his room.

Later, Zake said, "I have to sign a form at the attorney's office this Tuesday- which is today.

Zake came back at nine o'clock in the evening. He called in for absence at his workplace, then said to his mother, "I am going to run away. They have to pick me up. I will go into hiding."

Carmen stood her ground. Very firmly she said, "No! No! No! Once you go into hiding you end the rest of your life in hiding. You are cut off completely. There would be no connections, no families, no work, complete isolation. Not even I would be able to see you, and that would send me to my grave quickly."

Zake listened, slept quietly that night at home, and showed up in court for immigration, accompanied by his father and little sister, Zola, at nine-fifteen in the morning. He also knew he would not go back to the drug scene.

The judge made a ruling of deportation for Zake to the United Kingdom within four to eight weeks. He was also detained until the day of deportation in one of the federal detention facilities.

This was a day of sorrow for Carmen. Oh, the pain, sadness, grief, and ache that she was feeling. Had she not begged Zake to change the friends that he had? Carmen remembered the exact words. "You are the only foreigner in the midst of all of your friends. They were born here, their parents and fore-parents were all born here. They know people. I do not know anyone. Please, Zake, promise me you will change."

Her son just stood quietly with his head in the air. Carmen knew she had her work planned out for her. This would not be an easy task, but she was determined to stop this heavy, vicious cycle.

She cried. It was the most painful of howling, claimed their neighbors The agonizing wail that Carmen gave sent the most scary notes to those around. She screamed brokenheartedly, then cried again, and collapsed into a heap on the floor saying:

My son, my dear son,
This grief I knew was coming
But still was not prepared for.
This sadness was coming head on,
And yet the shock was unbearable.

I never knew what had hit me.
All I remember was how I felt.
My heart flew out of my opened mouth.
I prayed to die so I could leave this world
Of hurt, sorrow and painful woes.

So that you must know, my son,
The pavement you made was weak, broken,
And full of faults.
You never listened, my son.
Now the price that you must pay
Is worse than the actual crime.

So now, my beloved son,
The pain that this is causing
Is likened to a glancing blow through my head.
This sudden, quick separation
Has left me totally confused.

All I seem to remember was the voice of Zake's attorney. Quote: "This is a tragic scene. I do know it is a hard time for the family."

Carmen said quietly to herself, "No, it is hard for you or anyone else to feel what I, a mother, do and feel. This grief that is under my eyelids while crying causes such pain, my brain then goes into a very active mode. My mind was jumping. With my tangential thoughts and weak, limp body, it became very apparent that this was not a little problem. It was a catastrophic one of great magnitude that even all of my strength was zapped.

When this was finished, all I could do was sit, while preparing to recuperate from those draining thoughts that leave you very weak."

This big blow came without warning or signal, but arrived on June 9th into Carmen's lap with the weight of a ton of bricks that almost threw her over the edge of time. Carmen thought she was going to stop breathing. To her, the hour and time was here.

CHAPTER 26

On June 9th, Zake, along with his father Zaka and sister Zola, accompanied him to the immigration hearing. This was the day Zake would be taken away. Carmen was in no condition to go anywhere. She did not know what was going to happen. Zake had seen to that. Carmen only knew as he kissed her good-bye and said, "See you later." There were no hugs.

No cuddles,

No night-before talks.

What a horrible time for Carmen, Zaka, Zola, and Leah, Zaka's elder daughter, and Zake and Zola's elder sister, who was also as sweet as her siblings.

Carmen could not hold back, her tears running from her eyes, down her cheeks, and dripping down her clothes. These tears came anytime and everywhere. Carmen said to herself:

Oh, son, my dearest first born,
This final separation is liken unto severe pains
That overtake my now fragile body
With a barrage of beatings that control my soul
A son really needs a male in his life.
A strong, kind, and caring individual,
Who would teach him to be a man.
As Grande would usually say,
"Be a man, my son, be a man."

Lying in her bed with head elevated on her twelve pillows, Carmen started reminiscing about her precious son Zake and Zaka, her husband.

At least this time father and son appeared closer than they had ever been.

1.   They shared secrets.

2.   Their bonding time was usually on Saturday evenings until later into the night.
3.   There was a positive change in her son's behavior. He listened, and was honest.
4.   His eye contact was direct.

Dear Carmen pondered these things in her heart. She often wondered why Zaka had waited and watched to see her crumble at their son's downfall.

Carmen could still remember Zaka's words in their entirety. "I know what Zake is doing on the streets. I am not going to tell you anything. I am going to wait and see if you would die when you find out."

Carmen pleaded with her husband to tell her what was happening.

He replied, "No, I want you to find out for yourself, to see if you would die."

My young innocent son was around eleven years old at that time.

Carmen was also sure that at that age he could never be into drugs. He never stole, hi fact, he managed all of her bills, as young as he was. He saved her money as he deposited it into the bank, all at her instruction and under her supervision. These supposed atrocities could not be alcohol. Knowing Zaka was a heavy drinker, Carmen had made some rules:

1. No drinking in the house. She made it a point to search the house daily.
2. Weekly checks for Zake whenever he came home on weekends.
3. No gums or sweets a half-hour before reaching the house for mouth checks, or he waits near her for half an hour prior to mouth checks and mouth smellings, as well as burp smellings.

Carmen called her sister in Florida, informing her what Zaka had told her. Her response was, "Let Zaka know if he could not redirect this child whom is also his. He must be silent. All these years Zaka kept quiet. At age seventeen, Zake was arrested around four o'clock in the morning for selling to an undercover agent. He was taken away, sentenced, and incarcerated."

Everything Carmen had worked so hard for, she lost. So many hours per day; hours of hard labor, hours when at times she would walk from her home to her place of work, thus having two to three hours rest, then back to work with all the other stressors in her life, which was conclusive toward her nervous breakdown and other chronic long-term illnesses that she was saddled with. She now became a broken woman. She was very forgetful, but still fighting for her children. Carmen now became very disheartened, killing herself after worldly possessions, and at the same time neglecting her babies. Carmen cried; how she cried. This last bit had ripped her apart, and hurt her to the core.

Carmen continually told herself, "I really should have stayed in Europe. There is nothing but unhappiness in this part of the world for me. Over here in the States there was one thing after the other."

The most painful time of all was her neglect of her children. It was a time when they needed her, especially Zake. She, as a mother of two lovely children, whom she neglected as she busied herself with material possessions, things she could always regain as the days went by.

The biggest mistake she had ever made in her life was not having her talks as she had planned during their growing milestones. She had never even given him a stern warning or a strict talking to. She gave him neither reassurance nor comfort. With tears running in streams down her cheeks, dearest Carmen said to herself:

Dearest children, my joy, my pride, and my life,
Your mother did you wrong.
Again that she would always remember
Taking her right to her grave.

How could you forgive someone who should know better?
But know this, dearest babies, your mother craves forgiveness.
We, as your guides, are not all that perfect.
So now, my lovely children, we should take turns to share.

Our burdens we must share, especially in crises
Forgiving as we go along, the damages to others
As we tried holding hands with thankfulness
Being glad that we have crossed over that hurdle.

CHAPTER 27

Carmen often wondered who had started her son into selling and distributing controlled substances; such a bad disgusting habit for a young child to cultivate. This child never enjoyed his childhood to preadolescence and adolescence eras. She gave a big sigh. Crying, she kept shaking her head from right to left, whispering softly:

My son, my son, I have let you down.
I, a mother who has given you life.
Has never protected you as a regular mother should.
I never kept my motherly vows,
To love, protect, and nurture you
Until I am no more

Please, my son, forgive your mother.
A mother who was not there for you.
When, most of all, your need was great.
As I, your mother, realized too late.
Now I must try and get you through this need.
So be strong, my son, be strong for us.
As united we become, successful we will be.

With that, Carmen's tears began to pour. Oh, what have I done to my loving, young ones? I love them very dearly, and would always fight for them.

Now, in the end, while becoming a man, my male child has missed the joys through all his trials of becoming an adult.

Carmen, very adamantly, continues and insists from the time that things were going downhill she should have left with her children, leaving everything with Zaka.

Again she whimpered softly to herself, "I was so scared, dears. Your mama was always scared of the unknown. Even as a child, whenever I was placed by myself, my thoughts became very negative. At least I had the animals that would protect me.

"After fighting those fears, and all the other things that bother me, at this time in my life, I would be worse when it came down to me leaving with you two.

"What a vicious circle it turned out to be. For example, the aggressive life, and all the sordid, painful past.

"Now my elder child, my first born son, is now paying the price of my reckless actions. I realized now, nothing or no one is worth more than my precious babies."

Knowing Zake was progressing positively, what his attorney did next to her son was carried out purposefully to hurt her son, Zake. This almost caused Carmen to lose her life.

Carmen had a stroke which affected the right side of her face, suffering numbness on part of her lips, tongue, and gums, and swelling on the right side of her face, as well as pain.

This man was not an attorney in the field Zake needed. This was told to Zaka and Leah, Zake's elder sister, by her attorney. His attorney was not even known in his hometown in Dade county. His name was not in the special book that was provided.

Zake was charged a large fee in the thousands, and as he was always protecting me, cut that part of my inquisition short. Only Zola, his little sister, knew the cost. From then on, the vicious, unreliable attorney was never trustworthy. He never attended court. Perhaps he did not think it was worth his while.

The court file verifies these happenings. This caused a large amount of court adjournments. Zake was always in front of the judge alone. There was never any paper trail. All Carmen could remember was the frantic calls she had made to the attorney's office to remind him of his court date and his absenteeism's.

The replies that were given were:

1. He was on his way.
2. He is here in another department.
3. He is downstairs.
4. He had a prior case and would be there momentarily.
5. He is having car trouble.
6. He is paying a bill.

There were excuses from every area that one could think about. My son never saw him. As usual, he would arrive home with an adjournment.

Whenever Zake questioned him about his irrational behavior, he would return with:

We just passed each other, but I spoke to the judge.

The traffic was slow, but everything was okay. See you on the next court date.

Everything went well. I saw the judge.

This never stopped. My dear son went looking for another attorney, as he was:

1. Unreliable;
2. Unpunctual;
3. Unpredictable; and for his
4. Lack of manners

This attorney has never apologized for his tardy behavior.

Zake was not successful with a new attorney. Time was short, and everything was in chaos. The papers were returned to his attorney's office. Zake had a strong suspicion that he knew he was looking, but as he kept quiet, he also did the same. Zake claimed that his minister wanted to pray on his case. He told this to his attorney's secretary.

The attorney, realizing what Zake was up to, brought the case to a drastic end within a few days. On October 17th, after telling Zake he had to see him urgently prior to court on the 20th of October, 2003. he then told my son that the courts would take him away when he appeared in the court on the 20th. There was never why or how. He was going to be incarcerated by the federal courts. This man should have never become an attorney. He led my son to the part of misbelieving and distrusting anyone.

1. He led with promises.
2. He lied by telling him he had a chance.
3. He changed his pleasant attitude when he realized my son was trying to change representation.
4. He then acted like a carnivorous mammal, and with one large blow crushed my son dead.

My son was ordered by the federal judge without his attorney present, to be placed in a federal facility until time for his deportation. Of course, that evil man arrived an hour and a half late, and was reprimanded by the judge. Quote from the judge: "You are late. I have tried this case in your absence and ordered your client to be detained until time for his departure. I will reopen the case as you might have something to say regarding your client."

He stood and never said a word about Zake. Not even a plea.

Zake did all the talking, inquiring about his birth country, asking permission to stay in the community while awaiting time to leave the country, and asking how soon he would be able to leave this country.

Everything was explained to his satisfaction. The judge then closed the case. Zake was lead away in handcuffs, and away from his family.

CHAPTER 28

The judge reopened the case, but never changed his decision.

Carmen was in a state of shock when she heard the news. That was when she started to feel signs of a stroke. With all the stress she was going through, it was no wonder that Carmen became ill. The doctor ordered Carmen to take one tablet/caplet of Bayer Aspirin Extra-Strength daily.

The judge's ruling took away my son's:

1. Personality
2. Temperament
3. Completely separating permanently Zake's close relations with his family and friends.

This disgraceful attorney caused:

1. Severe pain to the family
2. To Carmen it felt like death-a sudden death
3. Hurt
4. Upheaval
5. This family was destroyed completely.

Carmen then said, "Our people of color are an evil, vindictive race. Even though they profess to Christianity, they are usually the most vicious, conning race in the universe, especially those with large bees in their bonnets. This attorney was in this category." Raising her hands into the air, then placing them at the sides of her face, Carmen became inconsolable. Groaning, she said:

This likened unto a death.
A sudden, sharp separation of part of me.
My heart is pounding, its rate feels like two hundred.
Oh, son, oh, son, o-o-o-oh, my son.

With that, she collapsed into a ball, rolling on the floor, pounding her little hands in a fist on the floor. Shaking her head from side to side, she continued:

He had sowed his time in incarceration.
He has paid for his crimes against humanity.
Now that mean attorney did respond to my son's idea,
Looking for a stronger and brilliant attorney.

He then, in a moment's pause, cut my child down,
Rendering him unfit for society in this land.
To know a sly, slithering snake is allowed such control
Causing an aching pain with a lash form his wriggling tail.

There is no heart, no conscience, no soul,
For one to cause such separation.
Such deliberate destruction of a mother's child.
That black rage that our men loves to show,
Will always be their downfall and cause them great losses.

Carmen knew she would never forget the 17th of October, the day her child was pulled from her arms. He was plucked like a chicken with feather scattering all over the globe, gaining momentum as the wind glides them away. Never to be seen again.

She continued with her musings. At least this time Zaka is playing an active role with his son. Going with him on his court dates. Giving support to his only male child, along with his two daughters, Leah and Zola. Carmen took a back seat this time. She was tired and believed her being there was a type of bad luck for Zake, as in his other cases he was found guilty in her presence.

This time, they were all together in unity and love for their brother and child.

The week passed quickly. Zake's attorney never apologized for his unprofessional behavior. He never offered to return Zake's fees or even half of his fees.

Carmen kept thinking of the sisters. They were very shattered at the judge's verdict. They both looked lethargic, and became isolated, withdrawn, and irritable, especially Zola, from being noisy, playful, and the perfect clown, was very quiet now. This was also the first time in her twenty-two years that my last pumpkin received an "incomplete" and a "CT" on another test. All of this because times were stressful. At this time, Carmen said she instructed Zola to skip the fall semester, waiting until her brother had left the country and things went back to normal, before she resumed her studies.

As for Zaka, he:

1. Lost weight
2. Complains of chest pain when going up hill
3. Has a very poor appetite
4. Cries continuously.

Zaka was very distraught. Carmen said she had never seen him in such a devastating state.

Leah was taking this the worst. As the eldest of three, she felt she had failed the younger ones. She never knew what they were up to. Also, she felt she never made herself available, and that there was no one-to-one with them. She always had a closer relationship with Zake. In addition, her son kept her so busy, and he would always take over his uncle whenever the uncle visited. Zake loved children and always took time to be with them.

Leah became very angry with Zake. How dare he ignore her. He never complained or shared anything with her. She thought they were quite close. She had to rethink another strategy to get her silent brother to open up to her. Leah was crying to break her heart. This even interrupted her work. She was given some days off by her boss.

Her mother, whom the children adored, took the shock of this news very badly. Dear Leah collapsed and took to her bed.

Leah's son, "Les John" never knew what was going on. Even as he was inquiring about his favorite uncle, the family decided that he should remain ignorant of the fact that Uncle Zake was being sent away to another country.

Oh, life could be so unjust. Carmen said to herself:

This country in which I have settled.
This country in which I have craved a new beginning
Has squashed my heart and left it dry.
The day they took my child away.

The court could have shown leniency.
He did throw himself on the mercy of the court.
Without a second glance of acknowledgement
The decision was made, no chance was given.

Away he was yanked to unknown areas,
Without knowing our son's history.
Is this justified to perform this dreadful act
To cause so much pain that pierces a mother's heart?

CHAPTER 29

The hardest thing for Carmen to do was to sit awaiting news. For example:

1. Awaiting news of her son's departure.
2. Hoping that the new attorney would take Zake's case. He did not.

This caused:

1. Irritability.
2. Watching and jumping at every sound.
3. A nervous wreck.

Carmen became very isolated. She stayed away from her friends and started to show signs of becoming agoraphobic. It was sad to see how she became. Carmen just did not want to be bothered. This mother had always placed her children first and ahead of herself.

She wished everyone would leave her alone so she could think about her troubled son and baby daughter. Carmen's children were eight years apart.

Carmen did not know which part of herself she must share with her children. She knew she would also give her life for them without a moment's hesitation.

Again she started crying. Eyes tightly shut, she said to herself, "Oh, what should I do? What should I do? They are taking my first born away from me forever, yet there was nothing I could do. This was worse than a death. The last of a human life. Will I ever get over this? Again, someone, a loved someone, a darling, is being taken away from me.

"All my life," said Carmen, "I have had things taken away from me. I have lost friends and people whom I thought were good to be with. I tried to put Zake on the straight and narrow path," said Carmen. "I even told him the consequences that would happen from drugs. I also pointed out that his friends were all Americans. Their mothers were all Americans with a history of southern ancestors."

Carmen had foreseen this. Had constantly pleaded and begged Zake to change his friends. Cut the drinking and drugging and pay more attention to his schoolwork. Zake was a bright young teen. When he applies himself to study, his grades were good.

"My son's bizarre behavior was pulling him down. His up and down behavior was pulling him down. He would pull his other friends with him. It was clear who was the leader and the followers. He would never utilize his energies into anything positive."

The only positive effort and gain from Zake was:

1. He always kept a job. He liked working and dressing.
2. Two years of college. He wanted to be a social worker.
3. A strong family support system.

On the negative side, he was heavily involved with the selling of controlled substances such as cocaine and blunts with pot. The law also added heroin. He was very streetwise and had a gangster mentality.

What I found in my assessment of the "black male," or as they are called, "the men of color" is that they think they are stronger if they demonstrated thug mentality by:

1. Their thug speeches.
2. Their walk and body language.
3. The clothes they wear.
4. Their hair.
5. Their teeth with silver or gold coverings.
6. Their vampire-style teeth.

The disrespectful side I could not understand was:

1. The boldness in which these children decided to be stubborn.

2. The disruptive way these thugs go around inviting these disgraceful people to come knocking at your front door, their clothes, and appearances very dirty and untidy.

3. Some could hardly walk and became very aggressive when redirected.

There is a very popular saying from my grande: If a child does not hear, he would feel.

Zake's unruly behavior almost brought Carmen down to zero. "There was continuous findings of contraband in our house," claimed Carmen. She had searches almost every day. When she did not find anything, she was happy. When she did find things, they would be hidden under any bed in the bedrooms, and scales and other signs of drug activity.

"I did not know what some things were, but I knew it was drug paraphernalia of some sort or another in our home. I know once I found a new gun with bullets. I took it to the precinct in Dade County and left it there, refusing the cash, but told the officers to give it to one of their charities.

"There were things in the letter box, in between the flowers, and under the welcome mat by the front door. Anytime I found anything, I would flush them down the toilet or throw them in the garbage outside the house.

"Then his friends would come calling. I soon put a stop to that as I threatened them with the police and Zake.

"I never stopped until my house became clean. This was a big job to keep my house clean," said Carmen.

"I then made a strict order and reminded Zake that no friends or company was allowed in the home. Nothing was allowed in my home that I had not bought. I do not care who bought these things. No dirty clothes were permitted anywhere in the house. No garbage was to pile up. No unopened parcels were to be left.

"I had to be on top of everything," said Carmen. "Whenever I complained to his father, my husband Zaka, he would tell me, 'What,' very nastily, 'I don't want to hear it,' 'You tell me one thing, yet when I ask Zake, he tells me something else. His facts sound as if it is the truth.' After a time, I stopped saying anything to Zaka. But I knew if Zaka had pulled his weight, our son would have had to toe the line."

Shaking her head, Carmen said:

The pain to find a child that is lost.
Sadness to know that things would have been better.
A slack father, an evil mother,
Could stop a child from doing the wrong thing.

I know a male child needs a strong person.
Someone to be firm and give lots of support.
It's sad to see a child turn bad.
Bad-as a pusher of that dreadful stuff.

You made your choice, dear son of mine.
The jump you took to disaster, my dear,
Caused the end of all your young ambitions.
It is sad to see a good mind gone to waste.

CHAPTER 30

"My son is feeling sad," said Carmen. "Only in this process he is also pulling me down along with him. Breaking me as well as him."

Carmen said she felt so listless. Her aim is what is good for Zake. What would be in his best interest. Carmen strongly felt that her son would do better in his birth country in Europe. He would have a new, fresh start to begin a new, good life. Making new friends-positive ones, and leave the negativities alone in his settled country.

In Europe he can begin to be a man. A man on his own, just as his parents did all those years ago when they left their native land for a new life in Europe by themselves.

Carmen does not want Zake country jumping as he is being encouraged to do. She prays he would give his birth country a chance, just as she had a chance and became successful.

Carmen said to herself:

Wipe your slate clean, my son, wipe your slate.
Face your new life like a man.
Your mom received her strength from your birthplace.
So can you, my son, so can you.
Make your own decisions.
Please be self-supporting.
Show yourself you can make a change.
Prove to yourself you can fight your battles and win.

Carmen protected both her children, fought their battles, and tried to give them everything. As a first child, she made sure Zake had everything. Knowing she was always on her own, she tried to meet Zake's needs. She even paid him for house chores and taking care of his sister, Zola. Carmen found things for her son to do about the house with pay so he would not go wilding on the streets.

Knowing that her field was poly substance abuse with acute psychosis, Carmen always believed if her children had tried playing tricks she would be there to intervene, coming with the strong arm. Nothing happened that way. When Carmen found out it was very late. She fought continuously with the demons that Zake picked up. She fought like a real boxer. It was a very hard time for Carmen and her young daughter Zola. There was no one Carmen could turn to. She hung her head in shame, depressed and hoping for oblivion.

As a young child, she often wondered what the adults in her day meant when some of them tied their belly, rolled in the fetal position, screamed in defeat, or screamed at the vast waste of youth turned killer. The loss of her son who once had a brilliant future but now had ruined his prospects for obtaining very good jobs in the city, state and federal government. He would not be fit for a good educational well-paying job that she had worked so hard for. She had worked hard for all her children to achieve and be prepared for in their future into adulthood to become good pillars in the community.

Zake was well loved by all, especially children. He had a very good heart, and was protective toward the females in his family.

"True, no crime goes unpunished. My son has paid the price for all his transgressions, hurt and pain that he has caused humanity. I, as his mother, never stopped caring," Carmen said. Carmen tried everything so that Zake could stop his negative behavior. She begged, cried, pleaded, and threatened physical force, all to no avail. The child would not, or could not, end his negative behavior. Carmen then said the more she planted her feet firmly on the ground, the more Zake became increasingly hostile, obstinate, defiant, and angry.

Carmen claimed the fighting wore her down, and in most cases it became a no-win situation, with complete exhaustion, with Zake coming out the winner with his instant gratification and his anal retentive behavior.

Carmen's plan was for absolute withdrawal from drugs, and was constantly on Zake's back to follow that mode. She dismantled the door buzzer so no one could come ringing. She kept alert and even called the police, reporting heavy traffic in the area of her home. She felt sad that she had become suspicious, but as per her grande, "Make sure is better than cock-sure."

Although Carmen loves her son, she is very angry at the way he has messed up his young life. All the young energetic plans he has lost.

Carmen maintains Zake is a loving, devoted child, who is kindhearted, gentle and has a lot to offer anyone. He does not bear malice, but speaks his mind with his two sisters. He loves his only nephew and gives him a lot of positive attention. "I only hope," said Carmen, "he would find a nice, kindhearted person to share his life." She prays continuously for this to happen, and even says to herself:

Son, before I close my eyes,
Please settle and find yourself
A good partner, rich in kindness and love,
Someone to care for you as you would do for them.

A good husband and father you would become,
Being a strong member of your community.
So, son, husband, and father all in one,
The head of your household you have become.

The long wait for deportation began at the correction facility. Their rules allowed for visits every day except Fridays, Saturdays and Sunday. The hours were six o'clock to nine o'clock. There were contact visits once a week on Tuesday mornings.

Now Carmen could count the stressors that caused such drastic changes to her way of life:

1. Uncontrolled tears.
2. Loss of appetite.
3. Very isolated, withdrawn, and nonverbal.

Carmen realized she could not blame anyone for Zake's troubles, as he was an adult by this time and must take full responsibility for the things he had done as well as the hurt, tears, and sadness he had caused other parents and families. He knew he had broken up some homes with his reckless actions.

Carmen had a strong suspicion that Zake was still selling outside of the home. This caused her a lot of stress, and at times she would be on her toes whenever he was outside the house, or late coming home. To say his past is catching up with him is putting it mildly. This is such a shame, for he is now walking tall, self-assured, and positive. Now he is being bitten very deeply into his buttock.

CHAPTER 31

This time my son has to pay dearly for the wrong negatives of yesteryear. This reminds me of one of Grande's Creole sayings, "You play with the pup, you get bitten by the fleas." An apt saying of what has happened to my first born.

Carmen then said in hurt and grief, "I never knew he would be taken from me in this way, but I guess it is better than death, which I do not prefer." Carmen then asked herself what kind of a mother did not have knowledge of her son's whereabouts, his friends, and their parents, and also what happens outside of the home.

How tough a love are we prepared to demand from our delinquent loved ones? What kind of demands would we make on them? Who would follow up if you were not there to reinforce this thing that is called tough love? Or would we just say this is to be enforced, and allow the enforce to carry out what was instructed and see it through?

Carmen realized she was having lots of mood swings lately. The worst, to her, was the continuous weeping. This was very tiring to her system. Then comes the dark moods, she now calls her blackness, and to her the smiling, high mood is Carmen's excited hyper-mood in which she becomes loud.

Seeing this, Zola would see to it that her mother was medicated so that she could get some rest. Carmen did not know what to do with herself. She knew she wanted to be isolated and left alone. She did not want to answer the phone or the door and did not want to see anyone. She could not make any decisions. She knew that would give her an instant headache. Even her other thoughts she did not want to be bothered with. Carmen felt like screaming at the top of her lungs, "Leave me alone. Leave me entirely alone."

Carmen had packed Zake's suitcase. She was told to call on Monday mornings to see if Zake's name had come up for deportation. She was allowed to pack twenty-five pounds of clothing in his suitcase.

He was also allowed to take up to one thousand dollars, which was equal to five pounds of British currency as per immigration. Around the time of departure, Zake's suitcase and cash would be taken to the embassy to given to Zake. He was aware of all these instructions.

Carmen knew she also had to talk to Zake, who every time his mother tried to have this talk, would get upset and cut short their conversation. In the end, she told him on his next call they had to have a talk.

Carmen had planned to talk to Zake about:

1. His conduct in Europe.
2. New company-they must be positive.
3. Work.
4. Paying his bills.
5. Saving, as he would be by himself.
6. Attending church as he was doing in America.
7. Reminding him that both his parents were from the Caribbean, and left their countries at very young ages, both survived and were successful.
8. He was to call her on his arrival in Europe. She would then transport his remaining belongings to his new abode and assist him in settling.
9. Carmen would remind him he was given a second chance, and he was to be positive this time. Wiping the slate clean and continue with his life.

It was agreed that the sisters, nephew, and Carmen would take turns visiting Zake, sending things over, and frequent talks. Knowing that Zake would be safe, Carmen decided it would be time for her to also restart her new future.

Shaking her head and blowing her nostrils in grief, Carmen said:

Son, son, son. Oh, my kind and gentle son.
I know you have grown into a handsome adult.
But along the way, I really wished you were trouble-free.
I feel so dejected with sadness in my heart.

I am trying to cope without you in your room,
Missing your noise, chattering, and off-tune singing
If only we could foresee our future
We would know our errors before we make them.

I do know, my child, you have the strength
To do good and become a very strong leader.
So make new resolutions, be content with what you've got.
You know I'll always love, support, and be there
Whenever you should need me.

Although missing her beloved brother, Zola was very glad he was getting on with his life and that all his negative associates were all taken off the streets, and incarcerated for crimes they had committed against humanity.

Now life goes on over here and as per Zola, Leah, and she are closer than before, and even little Les John, her nephew.

As for Zaka, he is in better spirits, but still feels the pain of this separation with his son's absence. His mood changes frequently, and his drinking is worse than before. Carmen says she thinks Zaka has very strong guilty feelings with the hurt he has caused Zake over the years. He keeps going over the past and all the hurt that he has caused.

Zake did hurt his family rather deeply, especially Carmen. Now, as he is older, it appears it has saddened him, as he is talks a lot about the past. He is trying to mend fences now.

Looking back over the various talks mother and son had prior to his departure and separation, "Let's be strong for each other," said Zake. Carmen replied by shaking her head up and down. Her son continued, "Mama, there was nothing you could have done in those days, or even say. I wanted to go down that road. "Dad could not have stopped me, either, even if he wanted to try. I was determined. Now I must pay the price."

Carmen became shocked and surprised at what Zake was saying.

He continued, "This is a new beginning for me. It is a good chance at starting over. Do not mourn or grieve for me, my decisions are of my choosing. I would not have listened to anyone in those days."

Thinking about her son's attorney, who never turned up for any of his cases, Carmen remembered vividly his angry, hostile words that he spewed toward her via the phone in a harsh, venomous, labored, angry tone.

"Your son is not wanted here. They did not want your son." I was taught one thing by Grande when I was younger, "It is not what you say, it is how it is said."

He showed anger, hate, and disgust in his tone. One could still feel the chill in his voice through the phone, telling me, a mother, the most disgraceful words I have ever heard from one professional to another. At this time, during the immigration and talk of deportation-my son was clean, and had a new set of working, positive friends, who spent their time traveling, going to different feasts and fests, especially on the weekends. He started to go on cruises, and then he came into contact with immigration officials, and the rest is history.

Now to have this attorney, this judgmental, bitter male to rob and hurt me, a mother, with this hostile venom, almost took my breath away. My son's crimes against humanity took place years before. He is thirty years of age now and has moved on in a positive way.

Yes, they were all given the title: Black man working, B.M.W., and they all were positive in that area. His other schoolmates that he had pulled away from.

CHAPTER 32

Trying to relax herself, Carmen sat on her sofa and began wool-gathering. She then remembered one of the letters she had sent to her first born:

My dearest son,

As you know, we have to be strong for now and the future. Always remember I left my native country eleven years younger than you, and so also did your father. We both made it well, and so could you. You have good values. You were taught to do the correct things in life. True, you made mistakes in your young life, as most people do. Now it is time to think positively. I know you have made changes and have started to show ways that you have grown, or should I say, "You are growing."

You must now prove to yourself, and then to others, what a strong young male you have become. Until you prove to yourself and say, "The things I used to do, I do them no more." I have proved to myself I am a strong person. Have kept and conquered my new goals." Then and only then you can say to yourself, "Yes! I am a man, a young man of color, who is accountable for all my actions, have paid the price for all the wrongs that I did, for the damage, hurt, and destruction that I have committed during my growing years to my family and neighborhood."

Remember, as your mother, I will always love you and will be there to advise you and guide you. It does not matter how old you are, you will always have your mother. You take yourself a wife, look at her, into her eyes to understand her. But remember, if she is not there, you will always have your mother, if I am alive. Remember, there is no love like a mother's love.

You are now starting out as a young adult. Go and show yourself, prove to yourself what good graces you were born with, your staying power, for you will not run away, but stay and face your new future as I have taught you, my son. Fight the good fight with all your might. Take time to know your birth country, and it will get to know you.

Call as soon as you are settled so that I can come over with your belongings. Buy a calling card to call.

Hoping to see you soon,
Your mom

Remember, my love for my children will never change. My tender love will always be there for all my children. All you have to do is call.

P.S. You do not have to call or talk to me. Just know I will always be your mother, will be close to you, and will always love you regardless.

Love and kisses, Ma

Carmen's mind became very active. Very tangential again. She settled for a short time on the last disagreement she had with Zaka. In no uncertain terms she told him when he asked her if she had heard from Zake.

"No," she said. "He is very angry with me as I would not cave into him. He is now thirty years old and does not need a mother. He never stopped with his tricks outside. That was too much for me. I alone did everything. There was no one to help me with him, and you do remember that." With a pause, Carmen waited for him to make a comment. Zaka never answered. So she continued. "I am tired and sick. Zake never listened, and no one should make promises about sending money for him to visit the West Indies, nor encourage him to return here via Canada. I have told the families over there not to accept or invite him to stay if he is only in Europe for one or two months. He is not going to return here so quickly and if he does, he could never work. And that leaves him with only one option-to return back to his old tricks. No, he is never taking me down that road again. He is going to stay in Europe, having gone over there. He must get on with his life in his birth country.

"Zola and I will visit and spend time at regular intervals, also Leah and Les John.

"He will also be in touch with us, informing us of his progress.

"He must not be encouraged to think he could stay here for two or three months. He must not be offered any cash gifts. He would be continuing with work as he was doing in the United States. He has received, and should be glad that he has a new beginning, a fresh start, and a chance of a new life.

"He needs continual encouragement. The thought of going to Europe must be brought up whenever there is opportunity so Zake must realize it is going to happen soon.

"He must be made aware that he must stay in Europe and not go country-hopping, hoping to go to various countries and settle.

"I know he is scared and nervous as he has never left my side or the family for any long, extended period," Carmen told her husband, "so please give him positive reinforcements." With that, Carmen wished her husband good-night.

Carmen realized Zake was very upset, and decided to give him time to cool off his temper.

"It is hard for me to think of him leaving my side," said Carmen.

"Here in the United States is nothing but big trouble. Lots of it. Since immigration took him away to await deportation, six of his friends have committed terrible crimes against humanity. They will each be receiving very long sentences. I am so scared to think what would have happened if Zake was with them on weekends. They are all in for attempted murder on two victims.

"As a mother, nothing is worse than hearing one of your children has gotten mixed up with some kids 'wilding' with serious complications and consequences," Carmen concluded whenever her son did anything wrong, she felt everything, and she suffered.

Carmen calls these feelings her strong gut, which to her, as a psych nurse, is never wrong.

CHAPTER 33

Carmen knew it was time for Zake to leave the country. Deciding she should have a break before he left, she decided to leave Florida and spend some time in California with a very close school friend. It was arranged that Zola and Leah would call her if Zake should leave the country. Sitting on the side of her bed, shaking her feet, she started wool-gathering, feeling her heart filling with grief. She closed her eyes and said:

Carmen, be strong, you must not break.
There are so many ways to communicate.
Be thankful he is leaving alive and well.
Full of strength, good health, and years ahead of him.
Mother, your strong son will be okay.
He has good strengths and strong, positive beliefs.
So, dear mother, be strong for your son.
Your first born would be safe.
He will remember all your teachings.
Our children do that when we are not around.

Carmen was having a grand time in California. There were so many activities, and her hosts did not give her time to think. She never even shed a tear.

Suddenly, everything went haywire. There was a phone call at eleven o'clock in the morning for Carmen. Zola was on the other end. Zake called from Europe. He had arrived two weeks ago on January 30th in this New Year, 2003. He now commences his path into adulthood.

Carmen felt relieved. Now she could take a break, for Zake, although an adult, behaved like a child. He was completely anal and turns with a snap if he does not get his way, and in the blink of an eye he turns into the sweetest, loving and kind person you have ever met.

Carmen knew she had to prepare to travel and post his things to him. Carmen can now say:

This was a new milestone. The end of an era of sadness, grief, lies, tricks, and unpleasantness. She wished her son well, good health, and happiness.

I have tried, my dear Grande, to be a good mother. I tried to teach my children in the straight and narrow way but to no avail. The eldest child was the hardest. The baby never gave me any trouble-that would be the girl.

I do not know where I went wrong. I really wrack my brain to see what I did wrong. What kind of hurt did I place on my children? I wronged them. I made wrong choices, and am paying dearly. The sins of the parents falls on the children, and my sins are really falling.

I think becoming a mother was a wrong judgment call. I am the wrong material girl. I never had any experience in motherhood. There were no role models. I tried never to use my past as a good role for childbearing and rearing.

Carmen claimed Zake took advantage of her as a single parent. He was very defiant, challenging, and confrontational, so Carmen would usually give him a hand's breadth of space away from her.

She knew in time things would get worse, for Zake had no intention of changing his ways. He is so greedy. Whatever money he received from his work was never enough.

He made so many excuses. He was never honest in his responses. He always got into mischief. One would say he has a magnet where negativities are concerned. Zake was never in need of anything. He always dressed well, looked well, was very handsome, and a good conversationalist. He was well loved by all.

Now he is alone, and having a fresh start. This will either make or break him. He knows he has my blessings, love, and caring. It's up to him to use his strength and motivate himself if he wants to be a man, be independent and make a life for himself.

In closing, I must appeal to mothers the world over. We must give our children tough love, make that decision quick and fast when we suspect any drug usage. We, as parents, must learn to listen to any suggestions and information that we might hear regarding our children.

I know in some third-world countries when one child is ill, suffering from any illness, the entire village gets involved. They will fight that disease or diseases until it is cured, at the same time safeguarding and protecting the other children. Of course, that village would consist of:

1. Mothers and fathers
2. Grandmothers and grandfathers
3. Great-grandmothers and great-grandfathers
4. Great-great-grandmothers and great-great-grandfathers
5. Great-great-great-grandmothers and great-great-great-grandfathers Numbers four and five are the grand matriarchs and grand patriarchs of the village. They are treated with respect, love and kindness by all.

Now I am getting on in life's years, and should I die, cross over, and return, my son would not be here to see me. He would never be able to lift, roll or even sing over me. Strangers, friends and other extended family members would be performing his role and other duties.

So please, mothers, hear my pleas, save our sons, for they are not as strong as our daughters, although we let them believe that they are. Please embrace them with extra love, always with that little extra, always with love.

I must stop now before I break out into poetry, those famous pourings from my heart and soul.

CHAPTER 34

Carmen realized that her past isolations, and ignorance's of life all helped in the breakdown process of her children mannerisms including their:

1. alertness
2. supervisory teachings
3. and milestone happenings as they appeared.

She brought up her children by trials and errors. Using her own judgments.

She really thought she was there for them regarding

a. food
b. help.
c. and need

Carmen never realized there was more to be done including:

1. More of herself to give
2. much more to share,
3. and making good judgment callings.

Carmen really believed as there was food and water also money for her children would not be left hungry.

1. These children looked alright: 2. Happy and contended 3.Very mannerly 4. Well behaved; 5 and needed nothing from her. She took it for granted that her children knew she loved them dearly, and they in turn felt the same way.

Sighing to herself, Carmen realized she had made a big mess of things that caused the ruination of her babies. Causing them to be labeled "A dysfunctional family" especially the elder of her two children. The male child who was trained for:

1. Master hood
2. Strength

3. Leadership
4. Making sound judgments
5. And protecting his sister at all times.

Again Carmen asked herself: How could a child so loved, turned so wrong with company not suitable for him.

It was hard to give your children good values, only for all of these to be turned, when they became in contact with someone else's children, with no proper home training who are selfish, and unperturbed about the wrong choices they have made.

She asked herself:

What kind of example would the younger generation receive from their senior peers who should really be of good standings

Turning to the destruction of her: 1. soul 2. person 3. and her character, Carmen wished she had stood facing her accusers, reporting what they were doing to her from age two to her late teens and adulterers; instead-

1. She took everything quietly as time grew.
2. Cowardly hiding in corners
3. Shy
4. Scared
5. And hoping things would go away.

Her son according to Carmen- found out in order to be accepted by his crowd of friends, he had to perform acts that would cause grave consequences, and sadness's for all,, hitting home the hardest. What was the reason to cause such negativities, causing so much pain,, hurt, and sadness.

CHAPTER 35

Carmen's past was sad and painful. Counting us all her troubled milestones, she came to conclusion her hurtful past was now passing over to her children Zake and Zola.

All of Carmen's vows that she had pledged to herself when and if she had any children appears to be going down the drain. All she wanted mostly was for them to be safe, secured, growing up without want she continued:

a. their company would be selective.

b. With their parents well known.

c. Her children's whereabouts and mannerisms would be well known.

Instead her, neglect and greed had really messed up her children's life. She suffering from her painful past.

Continuing with her thought:

Her son, this handsome, lovely young male, deliberately choose the worse for company for example:

1. There were always one crisis after another with these bored friends of his against the police.

2. The gangs fighting from one city to another, town to town, town to city. In each generations, from the tenth grade and up, without a word, thought, or signal these vicious fighting's begin.

3. There were continued fear for Zake's life, for example

a. Drive by shootings, also for our family members and other innocent children and adults.

b. Breaking into our house.

C. I always had to be a step ahead of Zake.

Oh the things our children put us through.

It was very sad how things have turned around.

Zake was never shot or want for anything. Carmen was so amazed that Zake had all that time on his hands, so he could become some sort of leader/follower in the world of drugs. Thinking these sad thoughts she felt:

1. the quiet which was as strong as before.
2. stillness in her whole being.
3. And chills that left her trembling uncontrollably.

Looking at her first born, tears began to run down her cheeks; suddenly she let herself go, collapsing on her floor she began to scream hysterically, her grief so intense, she was taken to the emergency room.

Her blood pressure was 200/150. They at the hospital worked on her until the systolic blood pressure, along with the diastolic blood pressure went back down to 140/90. She was then discharged back home the same dy.

Carmen's active thought process continued during one of their conversations which was with her "Pumpkin poots, and Poo-kins."

Realizing that she had helped so many young people, and yet again she was not there for her children.

Groaning, Carmen marveled at the way her life was changed. Without a doubt:

1. Her son was taken away from her. Again whispering to herself Carmen said, "This is like death." She often wondered if it was wise to have children. How can a mother survive if she loses her children.

2. Only Zola she was left with, and now more than ever she had to redirect her ways of teaching. Zola was left wide open for drugs, This child knew everything about the badly negativity , and the very good positivity of things.

It was a blessing she was-

1. Not abusing
2. Not selling
3. Drinking- in fact she was not involved in any kind of drug paraphernalia. This sweet child was very much into her books,

education, and into her own little world, unaware of what was happening, and with that any new changes.

Carmen smirked as she remembers the mischievous behaviors of her first born laughing more as he teased his little sister, tripping her when no one was paying any attention.

His little impish smiles as he played innocently on the household.

Carmen knew everyone loved her babies, especially the older generation,, peers, and the younger youths. As Zake called the younger generation.

The different aspects of Zake's mannerisms continued as per Carmen via her thought processes was that he- Zake outwardly would not appear to be distinctive to the naked eyes. He was always kind hearted and would place other people before himself, even when she became ill, he would place his cool hands on her forehead who could imagine this sweet child would turn into a dealer of drugs. The most destructive force one has ever known causing:

1. The killing and taking of human lives.

2. Breaking up of families.

3. Becoming a mother's dread and heartache.

4. Causing the early crossing over of mothers and other family members. Becoming a mothers pain nightache and heartache.

5. Even to the breaking, separating behaviors to all the homes.

6. On top of everything, making one's home becomes open target for these dirty, angry, vicious, disruptive scoundrels becomes very sad.

7. People with no remorse causing so much heartaches, violence, viciousness, and such diseases as Jaundice, brain damages, cocaine-crack babies P.I.D-Pelvic inflammatory diseases, multiple termination of pregnancies, low immune systems.

Opening themselves to:

a. tuberculosis

b. gross infections

c. infective hepatitis

d. The virus

e. and various other potential deadly bacterial infections

What bothers Carmen about being honest and also the truth factor was the blatant way Zake would shift from the truth,, even with eye contact on top of that, those soft convincing speeches mixed with words of love, quotes, and phrases really wins one over. With that young man one handedly knows where you stood.

When you hear words like:

"Mummy, My dearest let me give you a kiss." or ""Mumsie this is your boy child" or "Mumsie are you angry with your first born." I try very hard not to laugh, and would stay onto the important part of your conversation, so I could really grind him into any area of mother earth.

Now this young man of mine whom I love and gave life to is trying himself situated" his new word.

I know he is not superficial anymore. His honesty is hard to take, but I know this time he is telling the truth. He sounded completely different, more matured, calmer, and sure of himself. He returned to himself. His gentle disposition a plus.

Carmen know her son is continuously taking his time to climb his ladder for success in the correct manner. Remarking this to Zola and Zaka who seem to be in agreement with her.

Sitting by Zola's feet one evening in front of the television, Carmen blurted out a "No"

CHAPTER 36

Carmen realized she was again wool gathering as Zola politely enquired "No to whom or what." Looking at her Mother's face Zola saw:

a. Shock, so severe in nature, she was sure her mother would have collapsed if she was on her feet.

b. Her face showed extreme fright and horror, her eyes opened wide staring into space.

Zola said to herself- Had this been a bomb, she would have diagnosed her as being shell shocked. I became so scared Zola said,, I stood very still, unsure what to do or say. This was a different side of our mother, we all have seldom seen, terrible but true.

As a mother, as per Carmen- I still am nervous it is not out of sight out of mind - but intense worries, and thoughts about the past, the future, his new era, and where he is at this time of his life.

Being a troubled mother she worries all the time. Her children, she kept very close to her heart and by her side. All of these happenings has placed a heavy burden on her entire body. The constant nightmares she still continues to have. She had used every prayer and religion that she could remember, but now poor Carmen was tired, she flopped on her bed in a lethargic state. She move a few steps and paused. A note from Carmen- "Stop this now." "Stop this minute." This wool gathering was doing her no good. She realized when a troubled parent starts. to ponder about her children; these pains from thinking goes straight to the heart.

The tearing, gut wrenching remembrances that really divides her heart component into smithereens, telling what her first born gift said to her-

"Momma I cannot settle down until I have carried out my job of seeing to your needs, and making you comfortable." Bless his heart. Whenever he makes these big speeches, he leaves me in three states:

a. That he is saying more than two words. What is he thinking.

b. I am placed in severe shock and cannot reply.

c. This child is going to make me cry. Trying to bury me off.

In his melancholy mind when he was noted for his long speeches he would say:

1. "Mom I knew I did a lot of things to hurt you, and the family." "You took a lot."

2. Or: Mom I embarrassed and ashamed you. Do not keep blaming and hitting yourself, there was nothing you could have done, I had to get this out of my system.

In this vein this male young man would again continue:

3. You, Zola and Leah, are the most important girls in my life. I would always be by your side until your needs are completed.

This loving male, my son, who is my "Pumpkin poots;" would also have this mood of talking very rarely as the need arises he would make these speeches, which would really sound like a doomsday report. I must now continue:

4. I do not want any of you to be in want of or for anything. I have a good job in my birth country. I am doing well, so now I can be there for all of you.

Causing tears to run down my face, I would say this young man had a way with words.

5. My son continued, said Carmen- I really went too far. I am very glad I am not with that crowd anymore. I love my birth country, and am only sorry I did not come this way in Europe sooner. Please forgive me. I would always be grateful to you. He then said- "Look after Dad he is alone. He is not a bad guy."

I love you Mommy, Zola, and Leah.
"Peace and kisses."

Dear Carmen started some heavy crying, especially when she goes over these speeches. Her first born had indeed become the adult that he should have been years ago. He had spoken like a true gentleman, and like my father whom I could still hear faintly, I told Zake this quote:

"You are a man now my son." He chuckled "I love you Mummy." He always ends with those four words. It does not matter if he is angry, pleased, or the kind of mood he is in, those four words were always there.

CHAPTER 37

"You know; Carmen said to no one in particular; it is one thing to make a large mistake, another to realize, and admit you are at fault, but make sure there are no more, and continue with your life, making amends, and redirecting your life would be very important."

It is so sad that people have to be hurt or die; families destroyed before one realizes these things are completely a taker, a destructor, and a shortener of one's life. knowing that we as people hurt each other, especially our own races, who really scourges, acting as destructive beings and yes "Our people of color." Realizing now that my son was a "youngster of color," a very young person, when he was forced into this trade by a much older, meaner adult of color. I do remember his reluctance of going certain places continuously.

I really should have listened paid more attention to what my son was telling me. It was always good to pay attention to your children. Now, I am paying the price, and a very large one at that. I always tried talking and teaching my children to:

1. Know your enemies, their smiles are deadly, their eyes are cold,, they are coming straight towards you to either destroy, hurt or to kill you.

Carmen wondered, how could people be so stupid and weak, she even wandered what was the pull of these dastardly killers, everyone knew its addictiveness, its destruction rate and its smell of death, yet they walk with their eyes widely opened. Hands outstretched while their mouths and nostrils never closed in case they missed some of what's passing or smelling.

Longing for her son, and worried about her daughter, Carmen started withdrawing into herself.

Zola on the other hand just sat pretty not speaking since her brother's departure. Carmen knew Zola was very close to Zake, and although they were eight years apart, these years brought with its distance:

   a. protection
   b. care
   c. love
   d. closeness
   e. and togetherness

Carmen never told Sammie, one of her close friends: "It was Zake who really brought up Zola. He cooked, fed, made sure she was cleaned, even checked her home work. she grew up calling him "Ma Ma" as I was working on first shift said Carmen, that never bothered him.

He spoiled her in a good fashion completely.

I remember one night there was some noise in the kitchen. It was around two in the morning Waking her husband she whispered someone had entered the house and was in the kitchen.

Becoming alert he promptly told me to go ahead. He had put on his boots. I still waited. Then there was the smell of bacon, What a presumptuous thief. Cooking our bacon, using our gas and light this time of the night. While dashing into our kitchen of course I am in the lead, my scared husband in the back said Carmen - we saw our two children. My son was in front of the stove preparing bacon and eggs, while the two year old sat at the table fork in her hand, with her bright big eyes staring straight at us.

What had happened, this child woke her brother up saying she was hungry.

That was how he grew up. A kind caring child to a young man.

My child rearing was different said Carmen, it was by trial and error, as I had nothing to go by, I brought my children up to be very close to me never to trust anyone and learn to protect themselves, they had to stay far from families. My daughter listened to my teachings. My son grew up saying Mom I would always take care of you. My little giant was my great protector. the blessed child was always by my side.

Who could imagine a soft spoken, kid caring child growing up so drastically.

You know said Carmen: I have never heard my son cry even as a neonate, three month old, a much older young infant, an early teen or so I thought. He was just charming. We bonded together. He was nothing like the female child who was bold, stronger in will, fearless in spirit, and a little dare devil. It was strange how children have their own personalities as they grew older. As young as she was she still protected him. He being older protected her, mothered her so she called him "ma ma."

As she grew older their roll became reversed: Brother and sister, Sister and Brother.

She still was the stronger in spirit, very persistent and caring..

It's good to grow with one's children. I have with mine. They have taught me quite a lot, its like going back to school.

There were new words, new phrases, pronunciations, but most off all mannerisms. Some phraseology as renamed the same.

I do know both of my children did take to their education said Carmen.

Zake I know was not as consistent as his sister. One had to prod him continuously to settle down, concentrate and also take his time, his results would give good fruits for his labor.

The female child on the other hand was very consistent and always on the honor role from pre- K to the twelfth grade. They both graduated on time and went to colleges. even so, they do have a lot in common, for example:

1. they have the same weight.

2. They were both born on a Monday an hour apart, weight being 7 lbs. 12oz.

3.Four months apart on birth month.

4. My son was born 7:20 am on a Monday morning weight being 7lbs 12oz.

5. My daughter was born 8-20 am, weight being 7lbs 12 oz.

6. In two different countries with much love to share.

CHAPTER 38

This was all about Carmen. She was a mother in a million. Never having any comparison as a child regarding child rearing..Carmen was a changeling child besides being a loner, and could not imagine herself being successful in child rearing. Never the less, through trial and error she succeeded.

Carmen loved her children, and would be there to fight their battles for them.

These children did love their mother, they would protect her and would never let anyone hurt her come what may.

While growing, things were very difficult. Now with her children she was being taught to be a child, something she often wondered what it was like to be so happy and carefree. She had only seen this happiness on other families faces. Never on her face, only on her mother side of the family. She never knew her fathers extended families.

Her children whom she said 1. were gifts. 2.her good luck, 3. and good lovely angels, were sent to educate her their mother, showing kindness and peace

1. She played, 2. told stories, 3. did things together, and really enjoyed herself with her lovely bundles. 4. They educated her in current affairs, 5. Various histories, 6. Kindness, 7. the learning to trust, 7. togetherness, 8. the art of receiving and expecting kindness. 9. Folklore they learned together, and this came from the Dutch part of the family.

Carmen had a way of collecting things, writing things that go together, especially words of her children, their sayings and words that her children would use for pronunciations from the time they started to make speeches that she could understand and respond to. To her, Carmen claimed these were the best of times. She enjoyed every inch of their bonding and growing, in fact she enjoyed their little growth with them.

She could not understand how anyone could treat such prized possessions so evilly.

They were made to be 1. nurtured 2. hugged and cradled, she did that with her two bundles as she called them. Everything that she never had, she gave to them.

Physical redirection was out. Soft words were including:

1. Kindnesses
2. Plenty of positivity.
3. No threats.
4. Now and then a rare shout as you do realize these two bundles were all innocent.

Her son was a healthy male, very rambunctious, as all young males, go. He grew up into a sweet child, and now passed the age of consent, still a loving gentleman: 1. who loves his mother dearly.

2.Looking after her
3. Protects and shelter
4. Care, and spoils her with gifts, trinkets,
5. gifts she never had as a child, and even in marriage. He child, her male child son, and pumpkin poots, he would make a good husband whenever he was ready. Any son who was kind to his mother despite her faults and believe me said Carmen I do have faults,, as I am a paragon of Virtue, would tell me straight: " Mom if you could be so please to have him care for me" of course that throws me into a tailspin said Carmen, me; allowing him to nourish me,, what a laugh he was my elder child.

Now meet my daughter, like my son, is also the blossom of my eyes. 1. She is a cool young lady. 2. Very caring, 3.Careful, . full of love, 5. kindness, and 6. understanding, 7. lasting deviation.

My daughter, said Carmen, mother's me if I am not well.

I feel especially safe and secured with my two bundles. She is also very brilliant, as a wonderful loving wife. She would make a very kind, gentile, mate/wife for a positive person.

You see my babies are the King and Queen, of the future of tomorrow. Imagine such fine children devoted to their female parent - their mother, and still have their private lives.

Carmen pays tribute: Zake - for even though his behavior outside the home was negative, and he really needs strong reinforcements and support to concede his outside negativities. He is trying really hard to be positive in the communities.

She also says Zola will receive tribute from her for all the work she has performed in and around the communities.

1. This is a tribute to love,
2. peace
3. And charity which begins in the home.

This is in forever gratitude to my children who did everything to make my continued life:

1. peaceful
2. comfortable
3. restful
4. and in very good health they also find

1. peace,
2. happiness
3. be motivated
4. Show their strengths in every occasions,
5. be forever [motivated] united with each other;
6. have oneness
7. togetherness
8. above all be respectful
9. considerate
10 faithful to their spouses
11. children teaching them the importance of love.
12. education
13. respect to each other and harmony especially in the home.

I also asked that my children be:

a. Kind, continuing the way they were brought up by me
    - their mother.

b. If I should never cross over before them, remember me with kindness and affection, not as an order, but as they will.

c. Be there for each other at all times.

d. Share and be fair towards each other.

e. My son you are the elder of the two. I have never, took sides. I loved you the same. Be the big brother that you are and watch out for your baby sister, because that is what big brothers do.

f. My daughter even thought you are the smaller of the two, you must adhere to your big brother, watch his back for him.

These things my children you must do, again, not as I wish, but as you desire. I know you would always have me in your thoughts. as I would have you two beautiful and handsome children of mine.

CHAPTER 39

As was said before, as babies, Carmen would write all the saying of Zake and Zola.

Here are a few:

1. One Sunday evening my daughter received a call from one of her female friends. Unaware that I was awake, she then said, I was not feeling well. Quote" I have to go with my mom to see her doctor, she is not doing so well." said my daughter.

The friend must have also enquired about my hemorrhoids, which was a chronic complaint of mine.

Quote from my daughter: "I don't know I guess they must be chilling."

Imagine those little shrimps talking about my personal hemorrhoids in that fashion.

At around one year and six months of age our baby daughter could be seen with the chicken legs, even if it was not the menu of the day. It was a big struggle to take these bones of the chicken's femur from her, much less to find out where she was getting them from. We searched the house, but could not find any areas of storage.

Finally one evening we realized she was not in our vicinity by going into our bedroom there was our little angel her tiny feet protruding from our bed. her father going flat with his torch under the bed noticed and said: There she is under the bed with a stack of her chicken bones, probably deciding which one to partake of. Needless to say they were all disposed of.

"Children."

Something was bothering our son one night while looking at the television, our son suddenly stopped romping. Looking as if he was ready to do battle.

"mom." he said, "when you met dad, did you go to the movies with him."

I told him "yes."

He continued: "Did you have to go back home" he said.

I told him yes

"Did you have to go back home." he said

His father then said to me "you can try with those answers."

I then enquired of our son: "What do you want to know."

After a long pause he answered. "did you sleep with dad before you went home."

I replied with a very grim face. "No dear, I waited until the proper time, and that was after we were married."

Our baby paused again, and defeated by now said "Oh."

While leaving Florida our son had contacted chicken pox. It was drying out by this time. On leaving his aunt, she cautioned him not to be showing anyone on the plane his spots. the child, happy to see he was in big bird again, he decided to show off. In his best cockney accent he told the air hostess, quote - "Yook I've got the hicken pups." of course he did the show and the tell thing, that poor air hostess looked very blank and with the sweetest smile responded,, Quote- "How nice." He was around two years old.

My children took me through periods of despair at intervals in their growing up lives.

1st incident: My son the elder of the two, when it comes to his activities for example, the word: "Void" meaning to pass urine; we wanted him to speak properly. He came to me

son- "Ma, its coming"

Ma- "What's coming"

Running holding his penis, he said- "to pee, Ma, ma to pee"

Ma - Say Void sweetie, say void."

Son - Its coming, its coming, what' that Mama."

This child would or could never say the word void. To this day I have never heard him say the word "void."

My daughter the younger of the two usually performed the "wee wee dance."

She started with -

daughter - "Ma quick, quick mama, wory." while on her toes tippy toeing, then follows the famous "wee wee dance, those were all the words she knows "Tippy Tippy toes, Tippy toes tippy tippy toes, doing the wee wee dance she did.

This was Carmen's remembrances of Zake, and Zola

CHAPTER 40

Carmen also talks about her life, trust, and some of her past. By saying- It is so hard to know who to trust. What signs of honesty to look for, whom do you think you could ward off because you do believe you are very strong and could fight off the enemy or enemies.

Just imagine growing up with adults whom you called Auntie, Godmother, Great Aunt, knowing those females are the only close, trustworthy humans that you knew showed love continuously, honesty and freely, giving all of yourself, without asking for repayment or even a quarter payment in return.

I grew up having taught the following things: "You have to be taught to love, and to hate, you have to be taught the two."

Hate in those days was something very bad, yet no one around my era never realized:

1. How harsh
2. painful
3. mean and
4. cruel this one word - "hate" - could affect one's peace of mind, as my Grande would have said.

At another one of my growing milestones some of my mischievous friends and I during one of our showing off spells, decided to name all the painful words that came and meant the same as "hate," saying it with force, anger and meanness then comes the 1 loathing 2. rages of hatred, 3. The black rages of intense dislike, 4. The dark scowl with quaintness around the lips demonstrating with the various languages the using momentum of one's extreme, vicious, expressions.

I know the hurt I felt at my parents devastating break was compounded by various vicious, painful episodes of:

a. deceitfulness
b. extreme dislike
c. manipulations

d. with a young child facing all the guilt alone,

e. not being able to talk with anyone.

f voice an opinion

g. and was even very young to express herself in open about her feelings in rage at what she as a child had lost.

h. separated from

i that crumbled at her feet,

j reminder her in those days of "Humpty Dumpty" who could have never be repaired.

k. She saw her young life crumbling at her feet and never realized those pieces could never be replaced again.

She stood stalk in stance, confused, wondering, but never knew what was going to be the outcome of all these new strange changes or forms.

What Carmen now realizes and has also learned painfully, was the sudden brutal way that her parents had separated with an army of family members happy, to commit a killing, and shared the look of their success of their planning telling herself a home without a father is a home standing alone and empty.

This strong influence of the strong male presence is a must. This should really be a mandate by the courts for the many homes that are destroyed by the males absence as uncountable, with sufferance from their children, there really should be very large penalties, for a house of distraught. Why must the children suffer and these pains consist of:

1. Depressions
2. isolations
3. anger, black rage, black anger
4. suicidal thoughts and feelings.
5. Disruptions in the homes
6. poor role models
7. lots of negativities, and much more of unsatisfied needs.

It was amazing no one pays attention to the suffering children. What I learned from a friend was:

1. The hardest part of al these separations are - where we as children would be. Did these couples discuss with each other:

1. Their involvement with each other
2. Manage and staying together
3. their lives
4. Producing babies - their life like productions. Yet, as children are never contacted, opinions never asked nor challenged, we never had chances to voice any pleasures displeasures, nor even to take sides.

These now separated seniors who spent so much time agreeing and disagreeing have now decided to chop to the roots making a clean break without giving their children time to realize their ends are very near.

After all we as children do not really have any feelings, too young to understand the thought process.

Carmen could understand what had happened to Zake without his father, this strong man of color was not there to support him, have his back.

One thing I do know - a male child do need his father, or any male who would show kindness, encouragement and love, also be there for him, Zake really needed Zaka for his support, and teach him positivity. On the other hand Zola had me even though she still missed her father - especially their talks, support, kindness - A female really loves her father.

CHAPTER 41

Carmen decided to talk to a few of her friends, colleagues, and neighbors about their feelings of the single parent. Not really closing her mind regarding their sexes. First response was:

a. This was a single male parent. A very close friend of mine said Carmen. asking for his opinion regarding the single parent, and children with only one parent throughout their children/childhood/dependency by their parents.

He found it very hard even as a man to be placed into the role of a single parent. Looking back as he has now made it successfully, and the worst of times had passed, he now wondered how he, without the help of God got through those stressful times. Trembled as he said "A goose walked over his grave!" He wondered what these, four children thought of him - 1. a hard working male, 2. A male who was now mother and father to his three boys and one girl.

The mischievous elves never asked any questions they took it for granted there was never any mother, or as the only girl said: "Papa, you are everything, and know everything. He now wondered what she had really meant deep inside of her little head.

Carmen then realized and also remembers that children. Those little stinkers only see what to them are important, asked what they really wanted to know. These children must be really tunnel minded and tunnel visioned

b. This mother of two, even thought her husband was still in their house, he never took part in any activities in the house, or with his children. It was as if he was not present and was an absent parent.

It is very hard for a female to raise a young, strong, self-centered, stubborn male child who looked quiet, calm, but very deceiving, and times lies through his teeth.

This disrespector of females goes very deeply. Seeing this growing male child has learned from an early age that he was the head of the household as no man older than him was in his place of leadership.

Then there goes negativity, coping with all things that are shady, gangster habits, buying and selling drugs thus opening the entire area / his home with his single mother in dangers way.

c. Carmen also spoke to the couples who thought they were both independent islands. They were angry screaming's, shouting's, continuously fighting in front of their children.

Being in such dysfunctional settings these children became very unruly, doing the wrong things, leading into the world of drugs, robberies, fighting's, and inappropriate behaviors. Some of them grew up in detention centers, county prisons, and jails. It is so sad to see our children go down that way.

d. On top of all these said Carmen, she met the Grandmother with her four friends. She was now the primary care giver of this family, her daughter and husband had crossed over during a car accident. The children were now in her care. Granny as she was called admitted that her grands especially the three males who wanted things their own way. Not even seventeen; the youngest of these males being twelve were very disobedient, and she found herself in and out of the court system. Indeed she became well known in those quarters. There were truly a very disrupted, disorganized and dysfunctional family.

Carmen said she realized too late, that a home needs at least one strong adult, even if there was only one adult in that household.

What she also learned first hand was the consequences one receives after so many stressful situations for the most part of their lives smiling wishfully. Carmen hoped and prayed that she would never pass through all that shock, sadness, illnesses and running's with the police, courts, abuses, and beatings that she had gone through from her childhood to adulthood cumulating with her severe illness that she had suffered in her later years.

All her illnesses had been stress induced beginning with:

1. Her diabetes which started with Zaka's trouble with his womanizing.

2. Staying away from home

3. Spending his money on other women

4. Leaving the children hungry and alone.

5. The constant arguments between Zaka and her,, ending with vicious fighting's, him hurting the children to spite her. Coupled with that, she was then confronted with Zaka's negative wanderings, to cause:

1. Hurt to the community and its inhabitants.

2. Keeping very degrading, bad companies, those who had no intensions of becoming better and positive, carrying on with their bad ways fighting, brawling with themselves and the police.

3. Her son's paying back to society was the biggest stress from Zake to Carmen.

All of these was not good for Carmen's stress, Carmen had a host of other medical complaints, which ended with her having emergency surgery - major in nature. Carmen was diagnosed a day before her journey to see Zake with a "Ninety percent blockage to the heart."

She had to have a Triple-by-pass, the Surgeon told her it was to be a quadruple by pass, but their was one very good vein in her right leg which they used. This was made into a triple by pass; but she was told by her Doctors, they managed to correct everything. This was a stressful time for Carmen.

Carmen realized all the stresses she had encountered in the past from Zake and Zaka had finally reached its peak. She then remanished on the past and what Zaka her husband had said to her, " I am not telling you what he is doing outside." "I am going to wait and see what you would do whenever you find out."

How hard, vicious, mean, and nasty he had become.. He really meant to hurt and see me fall. To want to hurt me through my son, or should say, "Our Son." How could a man you spent all your young years, growing up into maturity just turn like that, vowing to hurt, just because he had suddenly fell in love with a few other females.

Men are really ungrateful.

CHAPTER 42

Coming from a family that was so distinguished in the community of her native land. Zake's behavior was a shock to Carmen.

Ashamed to let her extend family realized what was happening she allowed these things to be pondered in her heart. There was no one she could turn to for help. Shame is one thing a parent should never have if a child needs:

1. help
2. facing trouble
3. In terrible need of observation.

AA parent must always be prepared, just in case of any emergencies. Everyone in her extended families that had children around her Son's age were doing well. Some opened their own businesses, Buying up lands, buying houses. They all excelled in whatever they had studied for.

Her male was the only one that did not finish college, much less University. This hurt Carmen very deeply. The shame shock, sadness, and waste, did break her heart.

Carmen's relatives welcomed this sad news very supportably; such a great sigh of relief she felt, and everything came tumbling out.

She knew as her son grew older. She could not protect him, and really wished there was someone she could have turned to. This was all too late so she felt over and over that part of her was cut in half. Like a death, she felt the same as if her son, her first baby was wrenched from her gut this she tells herself continuously as guilt takes over her body and soul.

It is so hard to comfort a mother with a large portion of pain and hurt.

Thinking of everything, and her cancelled trip to Europe, Carmen moaned at the thought of not seeing her son.

The disappointment he must have felt when he learned by phone that she could not travel due to sudden illness. According to Zola it was the time that the world stood still. Poor little Zola had the task to tell Zake the sudden emergency surgery of "open by-pass" due to ninety percent blockage to her heart leading to a Triple bypass surgery.

Thinking back Carmen was very scared and apprehensive her children were in two different parts of the world, one would go around and leave freely, the other could do any, but could only come to U.S.A. as an emergency Although she was facing death, she did not want her son Zake to return to U.S.A. He had made a life for himself in Europe, settled and has started his new life in his birth country. He was now setting and doing well. Carmen suggested to Zola just play this down and tell no one.

Carmen remembered her praying asking the lord to look after her little prize possession - Ms Zola, Keep her safe from harm.

That was the first she had ever prayed.

The point being Carmen was a Buddhist and as soon as this life threatening catastrophe appeared her first thought were her children. This was time for looking after her babies, making sure they would be safe.

Immediately she closed her eyes in prayer as she says goodbye to her daughter. " Dear Lord please let me return to look after my babies. My little Pookie is all alone. "Please, Please my Baby Pookie needs me so."

All she could remember when she awoke was the shocked face of her baby, and tears running down her cheeks. Her Zola, her sweet little Zola. She was a brave little girl, a strong, warrior princess.

Carmen knew God had granted her wish for a second chance to become a better person, a better mother for her children and other children.

Gone was her faith in Buddhism. This was fight for her life and her children's. She also prayed that her husband changed his ways, and become a better person so the children could lean on him for some strong support. Her prayer was answered. She was alive, her surgery was successful. She knows she has to thank God. Never in her life did she begged for or needed something so badly and now received that, which she had asked for.

Indeed she told Zola " my dear daughter, you are my Queen, my strong little warrior, I feel so honored, pleased, and full of love for you, to be your mother. Always remember Mama's counseling's. you two children must always look after each other, as warriors do.

CHAPTER 43

What Carmen realized lately was her aptitude to avoid heated conversations her main theme was to be more constructive as she avoided any large confrontation, One evening Carmen jumping on her toes. For the first time in her life, and especially since her surgery Carmen stood her ground, and quietly responded to her children's father:

Carmen Don't you ever talk to me in that tone - that was when I was young and stupid.

Pointing to her heart with its incision said:: "I got this from you and others." All the stressors I have received all these years. I am tired, and do not want to have any more arguments with you. If this continues you would have to find another way to speak with your daughter goodbye.

Carmen wished she had adopted this positive attitude years ago between Zeke and Zaka. She would then been able to turn her son Zake into a positive mode; also save her children from such severe trauma, that placed her son so far from her daughter Zola as they were so close, even his elder sister Leah had missed him.

Carmen did not really like upsetting anyone, much less Zaka. He has a deep seated memory, bears grudges forever and his viciousness was always at the edge of some precipice awaiting to pounce always in the attack mode.

Does these things ever change.

Since her major surgery life has looked different in Carmen's eyes. To her everything has a purpose, and one needs to take time to think of one's actions, thoughts, and perseverances before making any steps for negative reactions. Carmen now has to redirect her two children re-more positive attitudes, and thanks for all they have received in the past and the present. Her councillings with her children especially Zake continues. At the moment Carmen keeps her fingers crossed as Zake appears to be focused positively, living a normal life with new friends and other positive family members.

Carmen still cries about their separation. They are mending fences, although trust is hard, she is trying very willingly to trust her son at this time, even if there are some doubts she listens carefully to what Zake is telling her, before making a judgment decision or calling. As for Zola, she is still the sweet child one could ever want.

Carmen continues: this child has never given her any trouble. Zola was always there for her, even as a young child. Her little sweet heart is her right and left hand. Carmen admits she loves them both the same way, and acts like a mother hen ready to scratch anyone if they so much as trying to hurt her babies.

Carmen claims she would always hover over her children; protecting them, nurturing, caring, and giving love continuously to her two pumpkins

As she claims

A mother's love surpasses no other. This love is better that one's new families without children. As Zake said "you could always find a new wife, husband, boyfriend or girlfriend, but never a new mother," and he continues to vow, even though this upsets her, that he would never settle down once she is alive.

These children have planned that they are both there whenever she needs them, then mumkins showed her love for them both, along with all her adoptees. Then mother Carmen loved them unselfishly, with all of her soul. Even those children that she welcomed into her open arms pay tribute to Carmen. She never realized how loved she was by so much people until she became so gravely ill. Carmen after her sad past, passed her young adult and older age milestones isolated, kept and protected her children from the mean and dangerous would, the only shocking thing was, trouble and misery came into her dysfunctional home and yanked her close knitted family further apart, thus allowing them to become adults before it was their correct time.

Opening her babies to the spoils of the world, corrupting them in different ways exposing them to:
1. Anger
2. Deceit
3. Trickery
4. Dishonesty
5. Hurt
6. Pain
7. Separation
8. Anxiety
9. Fear
10. Untrustworthy
11. Evil and meanness
12. Torture and venom with vanity

With tears streaming down her cheeks, Carmen wonders, all of these sufferings, and everyone expects a mother not to fight for her protection of her babies, for they would always be her babies.

CHAPTER 44

What I have written had to be said how could I just sit and watch my son's life go down hill without even a fight. To be ignorant is no excuse. A parent should find out everything about their children, by fair or fowl means. We have to learn to dig, even if your outer skin gets removed in the processes, learning the hard way to trust but keep a little bit of suspense where your children and concerned.

I although having a strong, powerful love for my children, was too selfish for material possessions, without thinking about the needs of my children. A male child really depends on both parents for guidance, love, protection, kindness and nurturing; the extras come when manly information's, strong male support, decision makings, and pep talks steps in, then of course the strong male in the house - that is - the father figure would step in and be there for the young male.

I cannot understand how anyone would say;
'It takes a village to raise a child, but a mother must become, male and female as a single parent, doing the functions of two instead of one, tearing herself in different parts, to maintain structural living, the correct way to bring up one's children.

Our men should take responsibility for the way our male children are raised.

The future of our young are at steak, our strong big brothers are not doing their jobs. The young are running wild. Drugs are everywhere and if no one was going to intervene in these negative escapades, the young would become locked up, not working millionaires, who would prefer to die while stealing, having drive bys, selling, or any other illegal, things they perform away from their parent/parents eyes, and form their homes.

I know I was never a good mother, as I have always maintained, and have really neglected my children, said Carmen I was a sucker for material possessions, never realizing how important my two loves were. Even to Zaka I have never tried to meet half way. I learnt the hardest way, of all, you must always have a back up; it's hard to go it alone; a support plan one must always have, even if it was never used. I must now bow my head in sadness and shame, because as a looser I loose the most important parts of my body, my soul and my mind, and that was my family, my immediate family.

Carmen said whenever there was blame, that -or- those particular coins would usually come in many pieces, and believe me, said Carmen, the majority of pieces came my way.

Looking back in remorse said Carmen, "I really do hope her family could forgive her for neglecting and ignoring them. She had paid a very high price for her family's destruction, and fall from grace; and more payments, punishments, and retributions would really take its toll on her.

Many had complained. Friends, very close ones who really loved Zake. Carmen knew they were genuine. The extended family members around the areas who took pains to hurt her and the children, they really, went to town with their broad cast with Zake's behavior, and mannerisms, when in fact as was told, Zake got into the selling trade from their hands.

The pain of trusting people whom you think are close and would look after your children's welfare, as you would look after theirs are very misleading.

Bitterly she said to herself. "I have really these uncouth bastards having not at this time persuade any positive goals, still doing

what they grew up doing in their roach infested holes -"Nothing,"-
"Nothing" - "Nothing." Indeed, they have not moved on, but are
still weak as water in no man's land.

In closing I must now praise my son Zake for all his positive
moves, new changes, and the positive turn around he has made with
his life. He had utilized this second chance congrads my son.

I did say you were given to me specially
I knew not what was meant
It was a long wait,
A very successful wait
When I was told you have to prove yourself.

Now you have my son,
And I am pleased,
To give both to a strong warrior,
Now you my warrior prince
Must continue with this new venture

Come hell or high water,
Just persevere my son,
Just persevere.

Done it this time. Drawing blood from her bottom lip, tears
gathering in her eyes she felt a loomy just like the atmosphere. One
should never make mistakes regarding her children. She had broken
one of her promises that was made to herself, and that was: never
let her children grow up like her, having the world on her shoulders,
each delightfully nibbling a small piece of morsel from her wafer
light little body. Now all everyone would be saying:
a/ this is Carmen's child
b/ like mother like son.
c/the sins of the mother falls on her son
d/ Carmen made herself
e/ She was nothing, now her son is nothing.

These same family members whose children were in worse positions that Carmen and Zake.

These little church mice dare to cast aspirations on her child. They that are ill bred, no class, nor good education, all hangers on, trying to nit-pick on her children. These people whose names are always in the newspapers with heavy crimes, against humanities, in and out of prisons for various numbers of crimes even including murder, have the gall after encouraging Zake, and egging him on, now turn and destroy his name. he was the youngest of them all, now.

ABOUT THE AUTHOR

Ce. Dey is also a writer of poetry. Some of her works soon to be published are:

Hurtings from my Soul

The Hurtful Eras: 1944 to 1966

For the Children

Clearing the Mind

Deep Feelings

About Ce. Dey

Born in South America, Ce. Dey spent most of her young adult years in Europe, where she completed the rest of her education. She arrived in the United States in 1980 with her son and daughter and settled in New Jersey, where she is self-employed as a registered nurse. Ce. Dey frankly shares her horrifying stories of abuse not only as a child, but also as an adult. In doing so, she says," I am Purging My Soul so I can go on with my life." As a registered nurse, she is good at what she does. She has found that not that much is mentioned about the seller/pusher of substances. They are the ones who gain notoriety selling. To her, they are the worse for addictiveness. That is the high classes of selling. She is also a mother of color and has passed through many hurtful, painful and unpleasant milestones. Being a mother she weeps for her son, a young man of color, at the dejections, insults and all of the trials he had to face as a young male growing up. He is now an adult and is taking his goals one day at a time as he climbs the career ladder to reach his heights.